Planet Earth

Author Shoshana Z. Weider
Illustrator Dawn Cooper
Subject Consultant Sophie Allan

Project Editors Abi Luscombe, Clare Lloyd
Project Art Editor Victoria Palastanga
Editor Hélène Hilton
Designer Sunita Gahir
Jacket Co-ordinator Elin Woosnam
Project Picture Researcher Rituraj Singh
Picture Researcher Ridhima Sikka
Production Editor Gillian Reid
Production Controller John Casey
Managing Editor Penny Smith
Managing Art Editor Anna Hall

First published in Great Britain in 2025 by
Dorling Kindersley Limited
DK, 20 Vauxhall Bridge Road, London, SW1V 2SA

The authorised representative in the
EEA is Dorling Kindersley Verlag GmbH.
Arnulfstr. 124, 80636 Munich, Germany

Copyright © 2025 Dorling Kindersley Limited
A Penguin Random House Company
10 9 8 7 6 5 4 3 2 1
001–348589–Nov/2025

All rights reserved.
No part of this publication may be reproduced, stored in or introduced into a retrieval system, or transmitted, in any form, or by any means (electronic, mechanical, photocopying, recording, or otherwise), without the prior written permission of the copyright owner.
DK values and supports copyright. Thank you for respecting intellectual property laws by not reproducing, scanning or distributing any part of this publication by any means without permission. By purchasing an authorised edition, you are supporting writers and artists and enabling DK to continue to publish books that inform and inspire readers.
No part of this publication may be used or reproduced in any manner for the purpose of training artificial intelligence technologies or systems. In accordance with Article 4(3) of the DSM Directive 2019/790, DK expressly reserves this work from the text and data mining exception.

A CIP catalogue record for this book
is available from the British Library.
ISBN: 978-0-2417-3121-5

Printed and bound in China

www.dk.com

Contents

4 Welcome home!

CHAPTER ONE
EARTH'S PLACE IN SPACE

8 Earth's place in the Solar System

10 Greatness of gravity

12 Searching for life

14 Looking up

16 Watching over Earth

18 International Space Station

20 Heading to Earth

22 Eclipses

24 Auroras

CHAPTER TWO
EARTH'S STRUCTURE

28 Forming the Earth

30 Centre of the Earth

32 The mantle

34 The crust

36 Plate tectonics

38 Rocking around the world

40 Volcanoes

42 Solar System summits

44 Deserts

46 Caves

48 Glaciers

50 Lakes

CHAPTER THREE
THE MOON

54 Orbiting the Earth

56 Robotic Moon missions

58 Sending humans to the Moon

60 Inside the Moon

62 The surface of the Moon

CHAPTER FOUR
EARTH'S ATMOSPHERE

66 What makes an atmosphere?

68 Exploring the atmosphere

70 Climate change

72 Worlds of weather

74 A new home?

76 Glossary

78 Index

80 Acknowledgements

WELCOME HOME!

Many people over many centuries have called Earth by many names.

The Romans called Earth "Terra". Today, some call it the "pale blue dot", the "blue marble", or the "third rock from the Sun". But the ancient Greeks knew it as "Gaia" – the goddess Mother Earth. This is a fitting name because it is our home. Home for you, for everyone you love, and for every human who has ever lived.

Earth is one of eight planets in our Solar System, but one of the many thousands we know orbit other stars. Earth is not the biggest, smallest, oldest, or youngest planet, but it is incredibly special because it is the only place in the entire Universe we know has life on it. Earth is a beautiful, ever-changing world, full of different landscapes and environments. Geologists and other scientists study Earth's landforms, rocks, water, atmosphere, life, and other features to unravel our planet's history and try to predict its future.

Earth is a globe, but it is not perfectly round – it slightly bulges around the Equator.

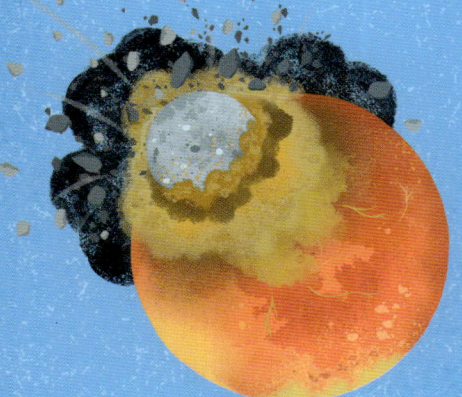

Earth's history

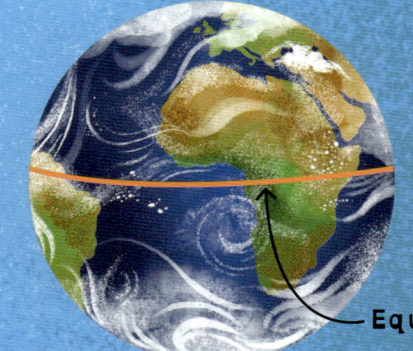

Equator

Earth

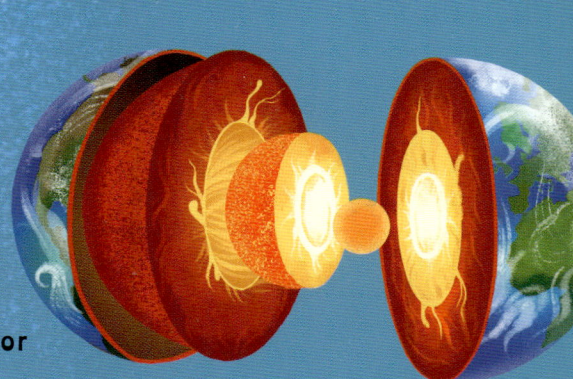

Inside the Earth

Water is the only common substance that exists naturally on Earth's surface as a gas, a liquid, and a solid.

In this book we learn about Earth's place in the Solar System and how life on Earth can help us search for life elsewhere.

So, come on a journey to explore planet Earth. First, we see what Earth looks like from above. We travel from Earth's surface, through the mantle, and to the core. Then, we gaze at Earth's natural wonders, including volcanoes, caves, and lakes, before we venture off to visit our space companion, the Moon. We travel through the atmosphere, then look at how Earth continues to change and how we can preserve it for future generations. Finally, we consider if we might ever be able to live on another planet.

Let's start our adventure!

Telescope

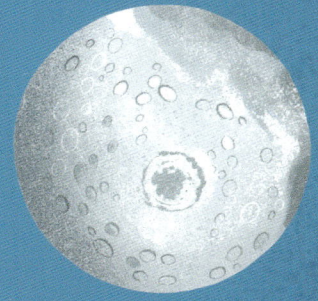

The Moon

Spacecraft

CHAPTER ONE

EARTH'S PLACE IN SPACE

The vast Universe is filled with many celestial objects. The Earth is just one planet among them, but it is our home.

Although Earth is separated from other planets and objects in space by great distances, we can understand our place in space in many ways. We use telescopes to gaze far into the Universe, and satellites to monitor our planet from space. These tools allow us to see how Earth fits into the incredible puzzle of space. Do other places have life, or are we alone in the Universe?

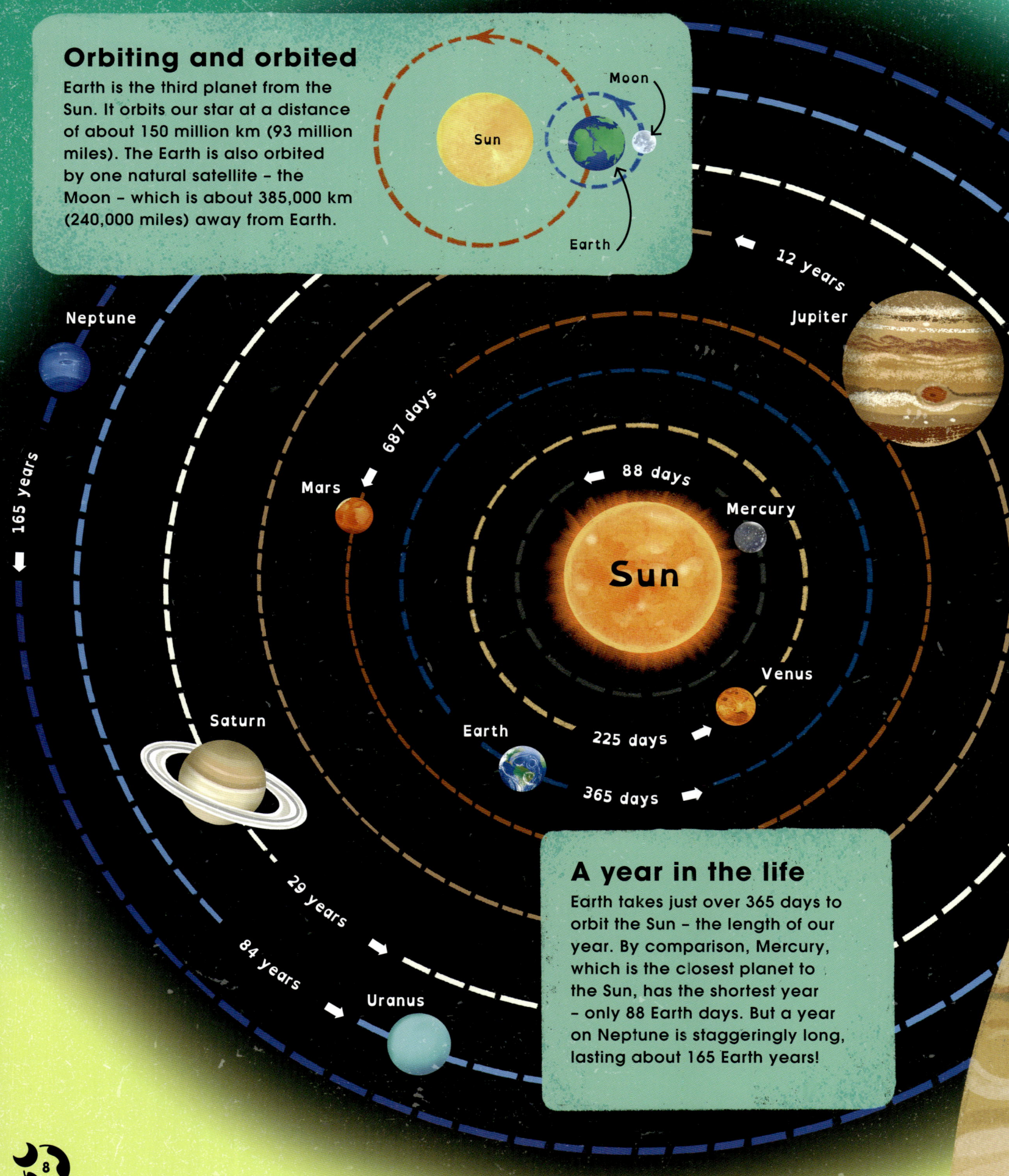

Orbiting and orbited

Earth is the third planet from the Sun. It orbits our star at a distance of about 150 million km (93 million miles). The Earth is also orbited by one natural satellite – the Moon – which is about 385,000 km (240,000 miles) away from Earth.

A year in the life

Earth takes just over 365 days to orbit the Sun – the length of our year. By comparison, Mercury, which is the closest planet to the Sun, has the shortest year – only 88 Earth days. But a year on Neptune is staggeringly long, lasting about 165 Earth years!

Earth's place in the Solar System

Planet Earth is our home, so it is incredibly special, and the Sun is the heart of our Solar System. Earth is one of eight planets that orbit the Sun. There are millions of other objects, called celestial bodies, in our neighbourhood, including moons, asteroids, and comets.

Solid ground

The planets in our Solar System don't all look the same. The smaller rocky planets – Mercury, Venus, Earth, and Mars – have solid surfaces and are found in the inner Solar System. The outer planets are very different. Jupiter, Saturn, Uranus, and Neptune are gas and ice giants.

Rocky planets

Mercury

Venus

Earth

Mars

Earth could fit inside Jupiter's red storm!

Sizing up

Earth is around 13,000 km (8,000 miles) across, making it the fifth largest planet in the Solar System. More than a thousand Earths could fit inside huge Jupiter, whereas little Mercury is only about one-third of the size of Earth.

Greatness of gravity

Gravity is an invisible force that touches everything in our Universe. It causes every object to pull other objects towards it. Even tiny objects have some gravity, but the gravity of massive celestial bodies such as stars and planets is the strongest. The force of gravity gets weaker as you move away from an object.

Earth's gravity also reshapes the surface of the Moon. It influences how wrinkles and cracks form on the Moon.

A gravitational dance

Gravity keeps our Solar System's planets going around the Sun, and the Moon moving around the Earth. The gravitational pull of the Moon and Sun together causes the changing tides in our seas and oceans.

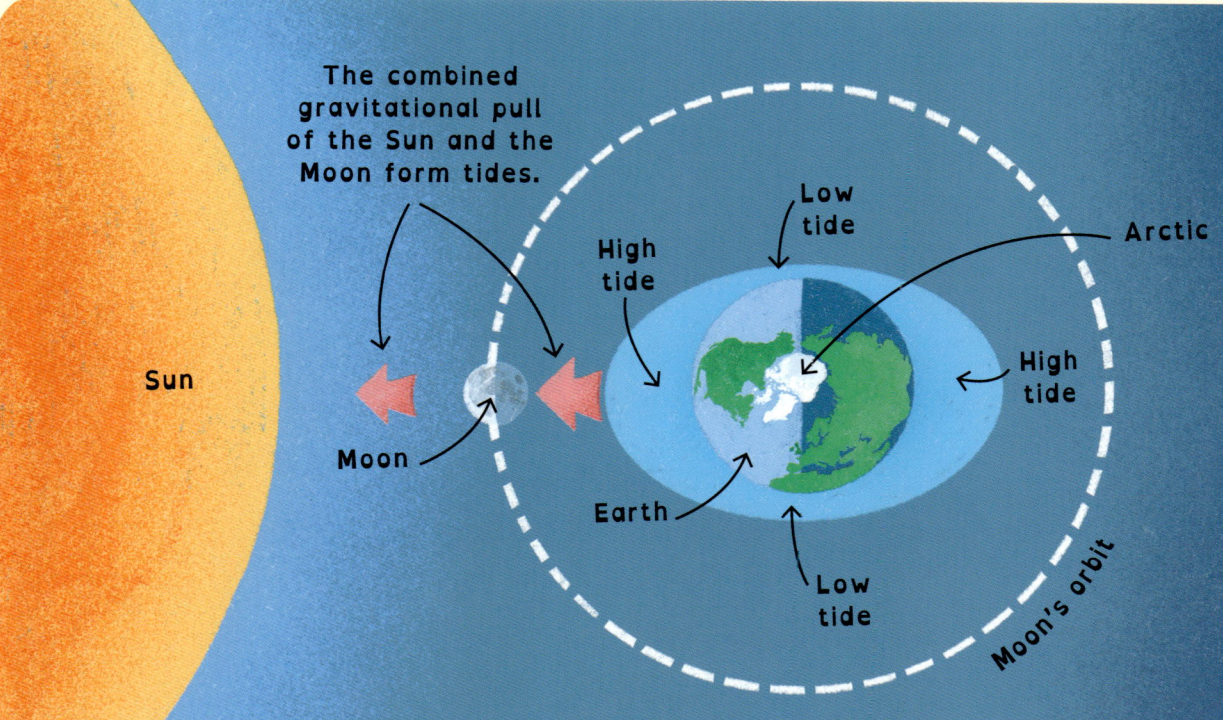

The combined gravitational pull of the Sun and the Moon form tides.

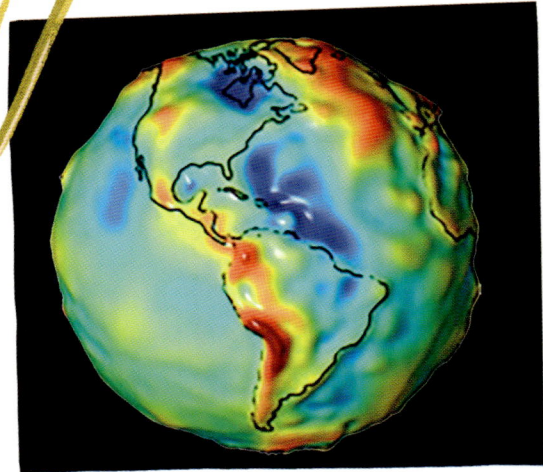

Map produced by GRACE. Red shows higher levels of gravity in places such as mountains.

Gravity maps

During the GRACE (Gravity Recovery and Climate Experiment) mission in 2002, two spacecraft orbiting the Earth measured how our planet's gravity varies around the globe. The maps help us study Earth's oceans, rocks, and climate.

Mars, (left) Phobos (middle), and Deimos (right)

Powerful force

Scientists think the two small moons of Mars — Phobos and Deimos — were originally asteroids that passed close to the planet. They were captured by Mars' gravitational force and ended up trapped in its orbit.

If you weigh 100 kg (220 lb) on Earth, you would weigh...

Changing weight

All the planets are different sizes and masses. This means they each have their own gravity. If you went to visit them, your weight would differ from that on Earth; for example, on Jupiter you would weigh 2.5 times more than at home!

Black holes have the most gravity — not even light can escape from them.

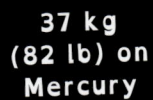 37 kg (82 lb) on Mercury

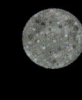 37 kg (82 lb) on Mars

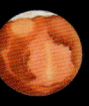 88 kg (194 lb) on Uranus

 90 kg (198 lb) on Venus

 100 kg (220 lb) on Earth

 106 kg (234 lb) on Saturn

 112 kg (247 lb) on Neptune

 258 kg (569 lb) on Jupiter

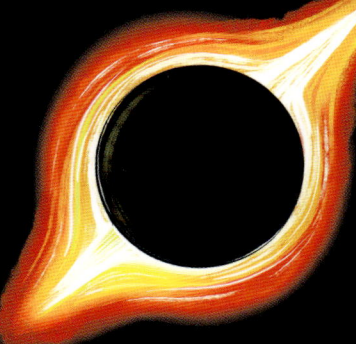

Searching for life

Earth is the only place in the Universe where we know there is life. But extraterrestrial life might exist and scientists study where we could find it. All life on Earth needs water, so the hunt for aliens often means searching for water on other planets.

Habitable zone

For water to exist at a planet's surface, the planet must sit at the right distance from its star. This is known as the habitable zone. Here it is not too hot and not too cold, so the water doesn't evaporate or freeze.

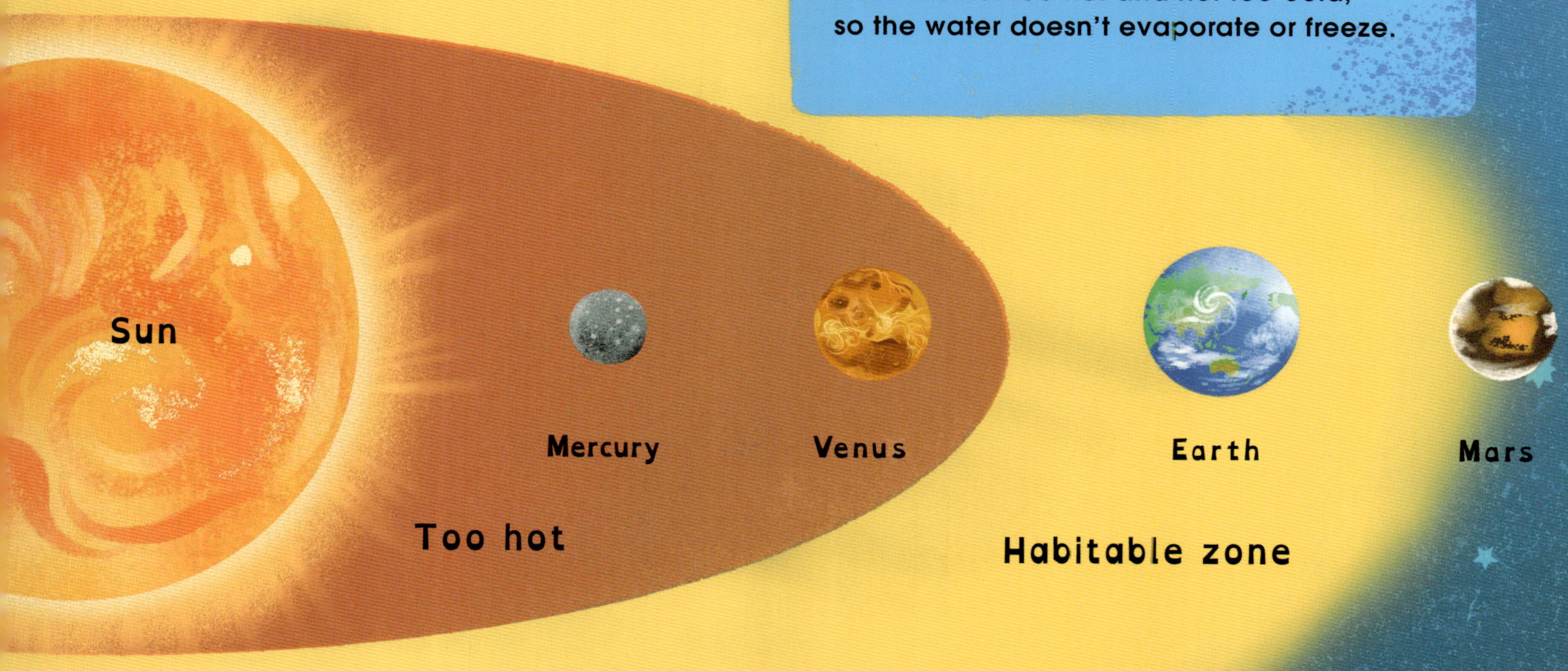

Sun

Mercury

Venus

Earth

Mars

Too hot

Habitable zone

Special, but not unique

Earth is the only planet in our Solar System's habitable zone, but there are millions of planets orbiting other stars in their own habitable zones. Many of these planets have already been discovered by astronomers, but scientists have worked out that there are many more to find.

Life's ingredients

Life as we know it needs three main ingredients: water, energy, and nutrients. Energy can come from the heat of a star. The basic nutrients that are the building blocks for all life on Earth are nitrogen, carbon, hydrogen, sulphur, oxygen, and phosphorus.

Water

Building blocks: Hydrogen, Carbon, Sulphur, Nitrogen, Oxygen, Phosphorus

Life

Energy source

Jupiter   Saturn   Uranus   Neptune

Too cold

Follow the water

Scientists think Mars once had liquid water on its surface. They also believe that the moons of Saturn and Jupiter – Enceladus and Europa – have large amounts of water today. These might be the best places to look for extraterrestrial life in our Solar System.

Enceladus

Europa

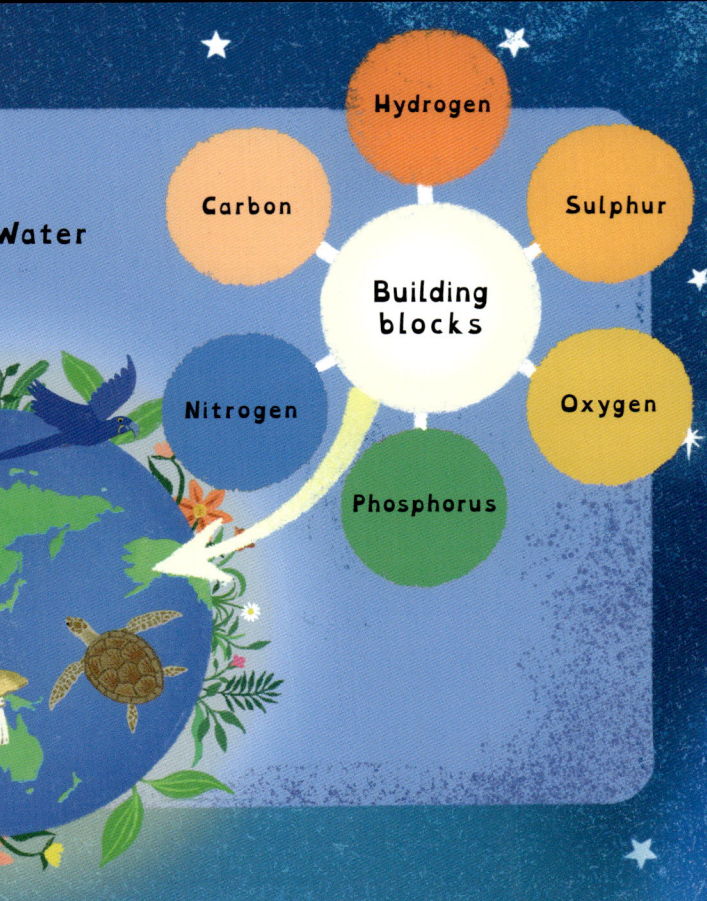

NASA's Europa Clipper mission will find out if Europa has the conditions for life to exist.

Looking up

Telescopes magnify objects that are far away. By using them to look at distant planets, stars, and galaxies, we can better understand our own place in space. The most powerful telescopes can see objects that are billions of light years away at the far edges of the Universe.

Early discoveries

In the early 17th century, an astronomer named Galileo Galilei was one of the first people to ever look into space using a telescope. He discovered Jupiter's four largest moons – Io, Europa, Callisto, and Ganymede. He also worked out that the Milky Way is made up of stars.

Galileo discovered craters and mountains on the Moon with his telescope.

Jupiter and its Galilean satellites, Io, Europa, Callisto, and Ganymede

The light we cannot see

Telescopes are built to study space using light. Some light we can see with our eyes, but telescopes also measure other types of light, including radio, ultraviolet, or infrared. This gives astronomers information about the space objects they observe, for example they can calculate the size of a space object.

Seeing space from space

Powerful telescopes can be placed in space where Earth's atmosphere doesn't obscure the view. NASA's Hubble Space Telescope and James Webb Space Telescope are two of the most powerful, and give us incredible pictures of the oldest parts of the Universe.

James Webb Space Telescope

Cluster of stars about 160,000 light years away from Earth, imaged by the Hubble Space Telescope.

Best views

Telescopes on Earth are often built on top of mountains that are away from light pollution. At these high altitudes, the atmosphere is thinner so the views of space are clearer.

When its construction is finished, the Giant Magellan Telescope, in the Andes, will be the largest visible-light observatory in the world.

Telescope observatories on top of Mauna Kea, Hawaii

Watching over Earth

Thousands of satellites orbit the Earth today. Many of them use sensors to watch the way our planet changes over time. The information gathered from these satellites helps us understand our fascinating home better.

What's the weather?

Satellites help with weather forecasts. Weather satellites collect data from the same areas multiple times a day. Weather forecasters track and predict weather systems, such as big storms.

There are around 10,000 active satellites in Earth's orbit!

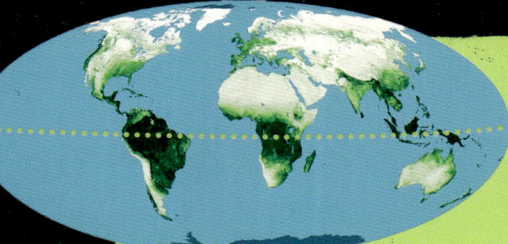

Vegetation in February   Vegetation in July

A green planet

Maps of vegetation on Earth can be made from satellite images. These show that the amount of vegetation is high around the Equator throughout the year, whereas in other places it changes with the seasons.

Moving Earth

Radar satellites are used to detect movements in the Earth's crust. By imaging the same spot at different times, scientists can see if rocks have shifted due to volcanic activity or earthquakes.

Satellite image showing movement in the Earth's surface at the active volcano, Kīlauea, in Hawaii

Measuring magnetism

Earth's magnetic field can also be measured by satellites. They help us understand the shape and structure of the magnetic field around our planet.

International Space Station

The International Space Station (ISS) is a huge space research station. It orbits the Earth around 400 km (250 miles) above us and circles the Earth about 16 times a day. Many different countries work together to look after the ISS.

Just like home
Building the ISS started in 1998 and took years to finish. It is now the size of a six-bedroom house and, just like a home, is divided into sections including bedrooms, bathrooms, a gym, and a kitchen.

NASA astronaut Loral O'Hara exercises on a cycle.

Long stays
People have been living on the ISS for almost 25 years – some have stayed there for more than a year at a time. These long stays on the ISS help us learn how astronauts may cope with long journeys to places like Mars.

NASA astronaut Peggy Whitson spent a total of 665 days in space.

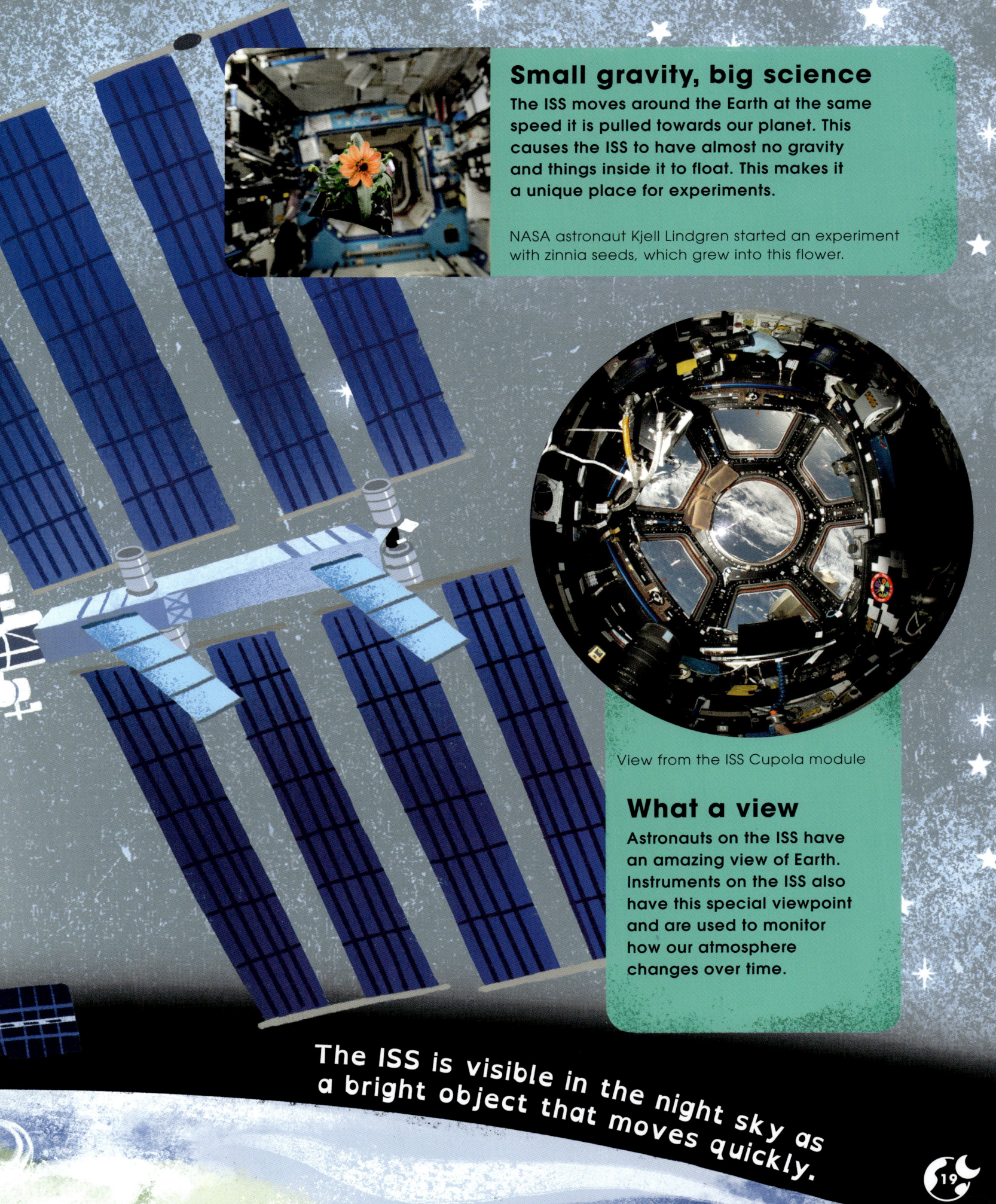

Small gravity, big science

The ISS moves around the Earth at the same speed it is pulled towards our planet. This causes the ISS to have almost no gravity and things inside it to float. This makes it a unique place for experiments.

NASA astronaut Kjell Lindgren started an experiment with zinnia seeds, which grew into this flower.

View from the ISS Cupola module

What a view

Astronauts on the ISS have an amazing view of Earth. Instruments on the ISS also have this special viewpoint and are used to monitor how our atmosphere changes over time.

The ISS is visible in the night sky as a bright object that moves quickly.

Heading to Earth

Asteroids are small, rocky objects that orbit the Sun. The largest is about 500 km (310 miles) wide, whereas the smallest asteroids are only a few metres across. Many asteroids in our Solar System form a band, known as the Main Asteroid Belt, which lies between the orbits of Mars and Jupiter.

Collision course

The orbits of some asteroids put them on a collision course with planets, including Earth. Many of the craters we see on the Moon are records of asteroid impacts. We can learn about these asteroids by studying the craters they made.

Meteor Crater in Arizona, USA, was created by an asteroid impact.

Meteorites are the pieces of rock that are left after an asteroid impacts Earth.

Cosmic rain

Tiny pieces of dust, called cosmic dust, are always falling through our atmosphere. These dust particles are less than a millimetre (0.04 in) in size and come from all over the Solar System and beyond.

Microscope image of a cosmic dust particle

Dinosaur killer

The Chicxulub crater, under the sea near Mexico, is the scar left by an asteroid, about 10 km (6 miles) in diameter that hit Earth about 66 million years ago. The devastating impact led to the extinction of the dinosaurs.

The huge asteroid wiped out about 75 per cent of all animal species on Earth.

Water delivery

Scientists still aren't sure where Earth got all its water from. Some think that asteroids and comets may have delivered ice and water to our planet billions of years ago. Missions sent to explore asteroids and comets can help us test this idea.

ESA's Rosetta spacecraft visited and studied the Comet 67P/Churyumov-Gerasimenko, which releases water vapour from its icy surface.

Eclipses

Sometimes the Earth, Moon, and Sun perfectly line up so that the Moon blocks the face of the Sun. This is called a total solar eclipse. This special moment occurs because the Sun is 400 times bigger than the Moon and also 400 times further away.

Rare events

The orbits of the Earth around the Sun and the Moon around the Earth are not perfectly circular or perfectly on the same horizontal level. This means that we don't see a total solar eclipse every month – they happen about every 18 months.

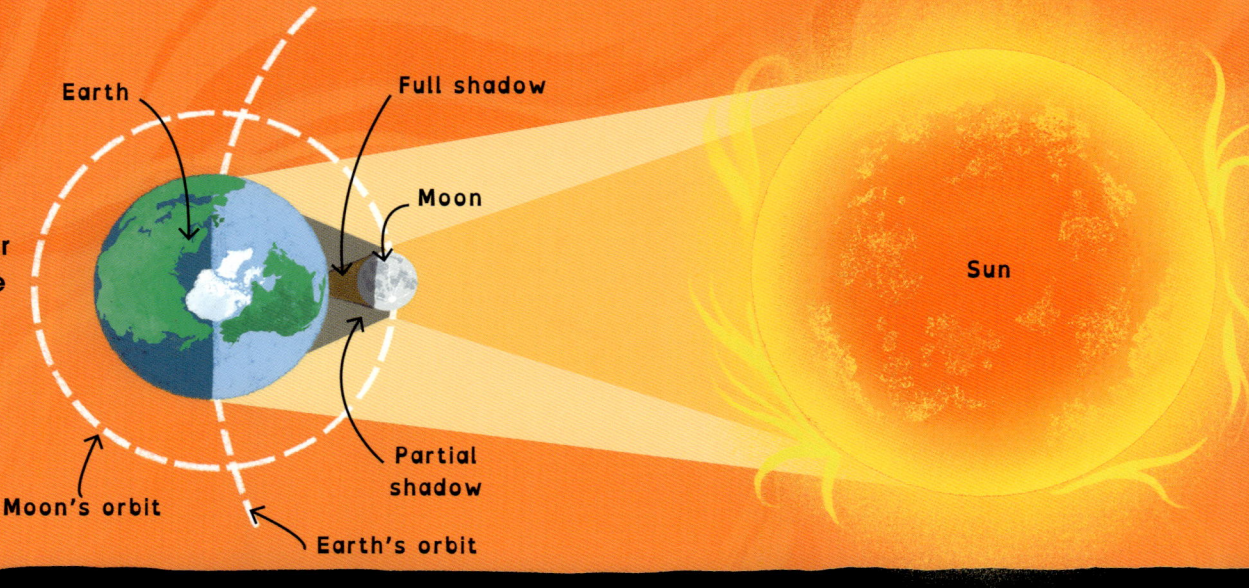

Blocking out the Sun

Before eclipse

25% eclipsed

50% eclipsed

The view from Mars

No other planet in our Solar System can experience a total solar eclipse like we do on Earth. However, cameras on several Mars rovers have captured images and videos of its two moons, Deimos and Phobos, crossing in front of the Sun.

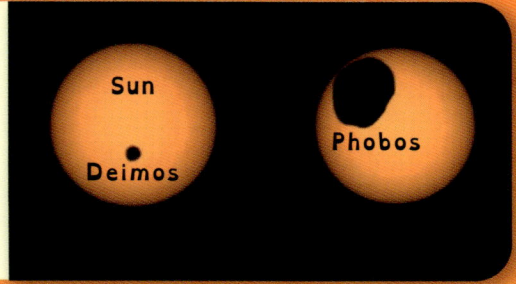

Blood Moon

On Earth, we also see total lunar eclipses. These happen when a full Moon enters the Earth's shadow, about every six months. During a total lunar eclipse the Moon darkens to a beautiful blood red.

Moon during a total lunar eclipse.

75% eclipsed

Total eclipse begins

Total eclipse

Solar science

The only part of the Sun that is visible during a total solar eclipse is the corona (the Sun's atmosphere). This means solar eclipses are great times for scientists to study the outer parts of the Sun and the solar wind (a stream of charged particles that flows out of the Sun).

Auroras

During storms on the Sun, fast-moving, electrically charged particles are released and sent out into space. Some travel towards Earth. Earth's magnetic field mostly stops these particles from entering our atmosphere. However, near the North and South Poles the particles crash into the atmosphere's gas and produce colourful lights, called auroras.

Storm cycles

Auroras can happen at any time, but are most common when the Sun has lots of storms. This occurs every 11 years, during a solar maximum, which is when the Sun's cycle is most active. Auroras caused by the strongest solar storms can even be seen away from Earth's poles.

Lights of many colours

Auroras – also called northern and southern lights – come in many different colours and shapes. The most common colour is green, caused by oxygen. Nitrogen in the atmosphere can also cause the lights to glow in purple, blue, or pink. Red auroras are rare, but they do also happen.

As well as beautiful colours, auroras can make crackling, whistling, and hissing sounds.

Solar flares are explosions of energy at the Sun's surface.

On other worlds

Earth is not the only planet where auroras take place. Using telescopes and spacecraft, auroras have been seen at Jupiter, Saturn, Uranus, and Neptune. NASA's MAVEN spacecraft orbiting Mars has also measured many auroras taking place in Mars' thin atmosphere.

Auroras on Saturn

The view from space

Astronauts on the International Space Station (ISS) sometimes get to fly through auroras! The ISS orbits between 370 and 460 km (230 and 285 miles) above the Earth. Auroras occur at these same heights, giving the astronauts a unique view of the phenomenon.

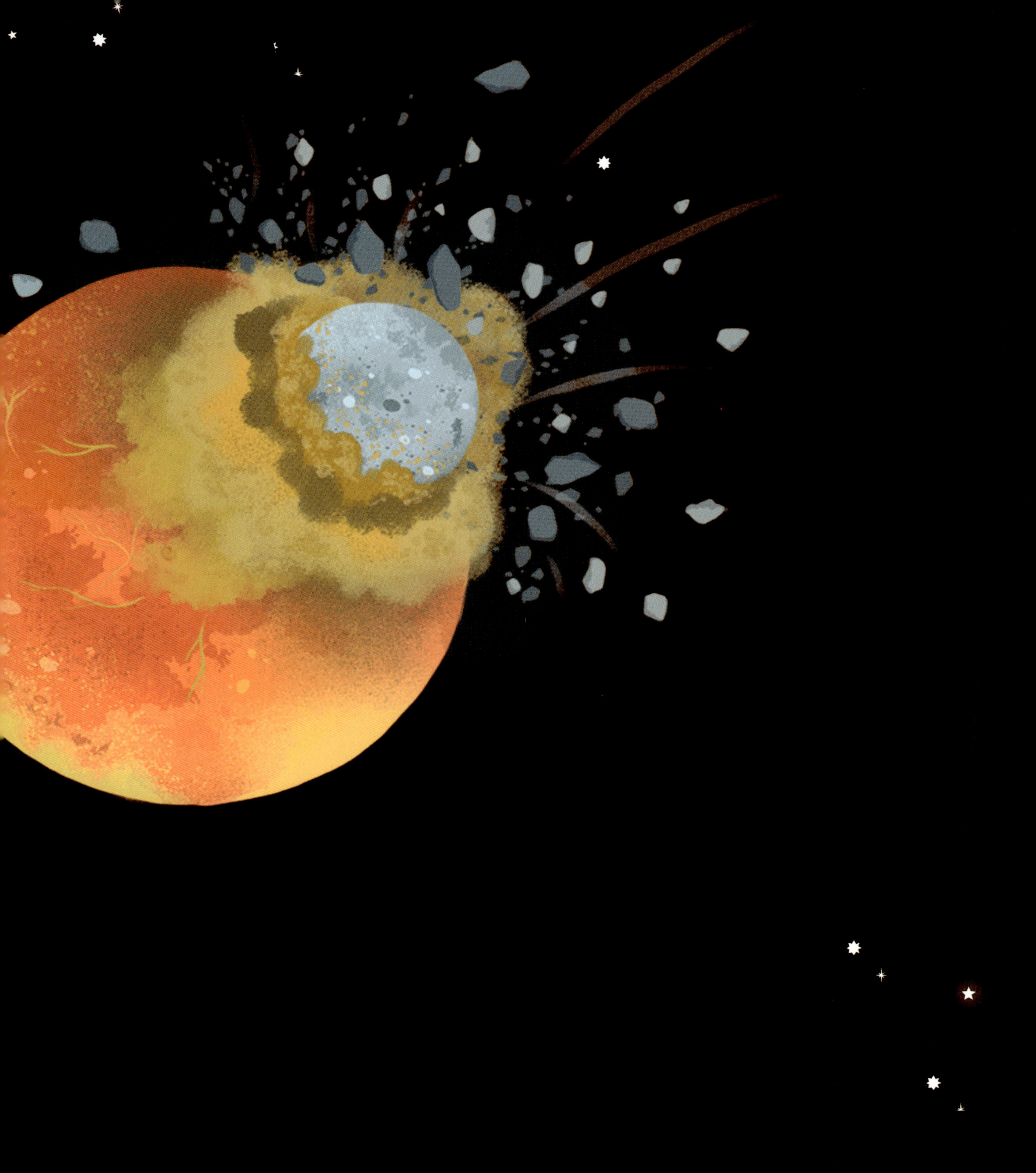

CHAPTER TWO

EARTH'S STRUCTURE

Earth is a fascinating, ever-changing planet. Unlike any other in our Solar System, it is a world covered by water.

By learning about the Earth's layered structure and its geological features, we can understand how our home planet was formed. Geologists find clues about the Earth's past on its surface, the crust. They study the Earth's rock cycle, its mountains, volcanoes, and deserts. However, our planet is unique: it is home to water in many forms, including oceans, glaciers, and lakes.

Forming the Earth

The Earth started to form more than 4.5 billion years ago. Like all the planets, the Earth came together from a cloud of gas and dust swirling around the young Sun. Gradually, larger and larger chunks of material stuck together until eventually, the Earth was born.

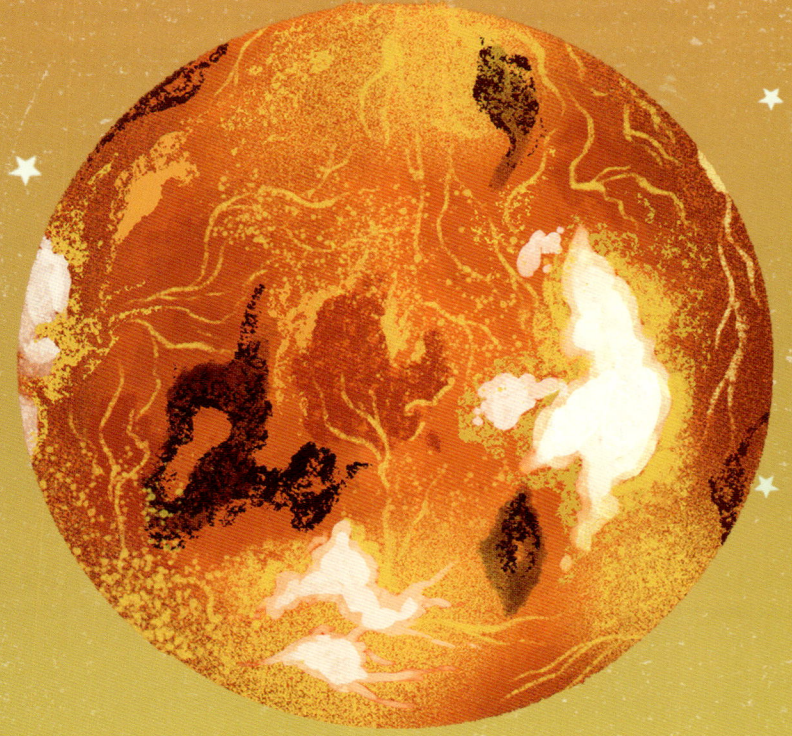

Starting out

As the Earth cooled, the magma began to solidify. In this process, material that was heavy sank to the middle of the planet to make the core. Lighter materials floated to the top of the ocean of magma to create a crust.

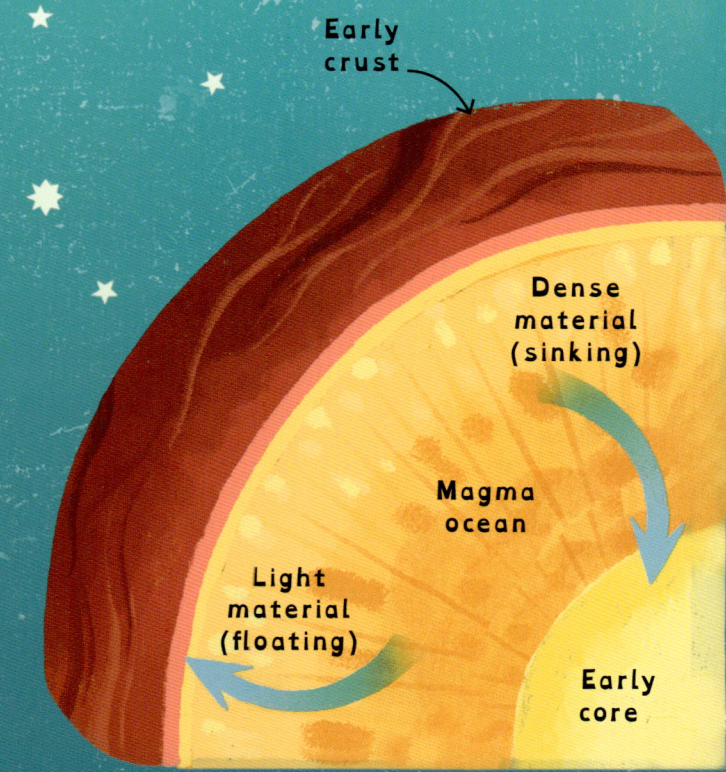

Magma world

The oldest part of Earth's history lasted about half a billion years and is called the Hadean Eon. It's hard to know what the Earth was like then, but it was extremely hot and most of the planet was made of magma (melted rock).

Moon birth

The Moon was created very early in Earth's history during the Hadean Eon when another planet-sized celestial object, called Theia, collided with early Earth. The debris from this giant impact came back together in orbit around the Earth and formed the Moon.

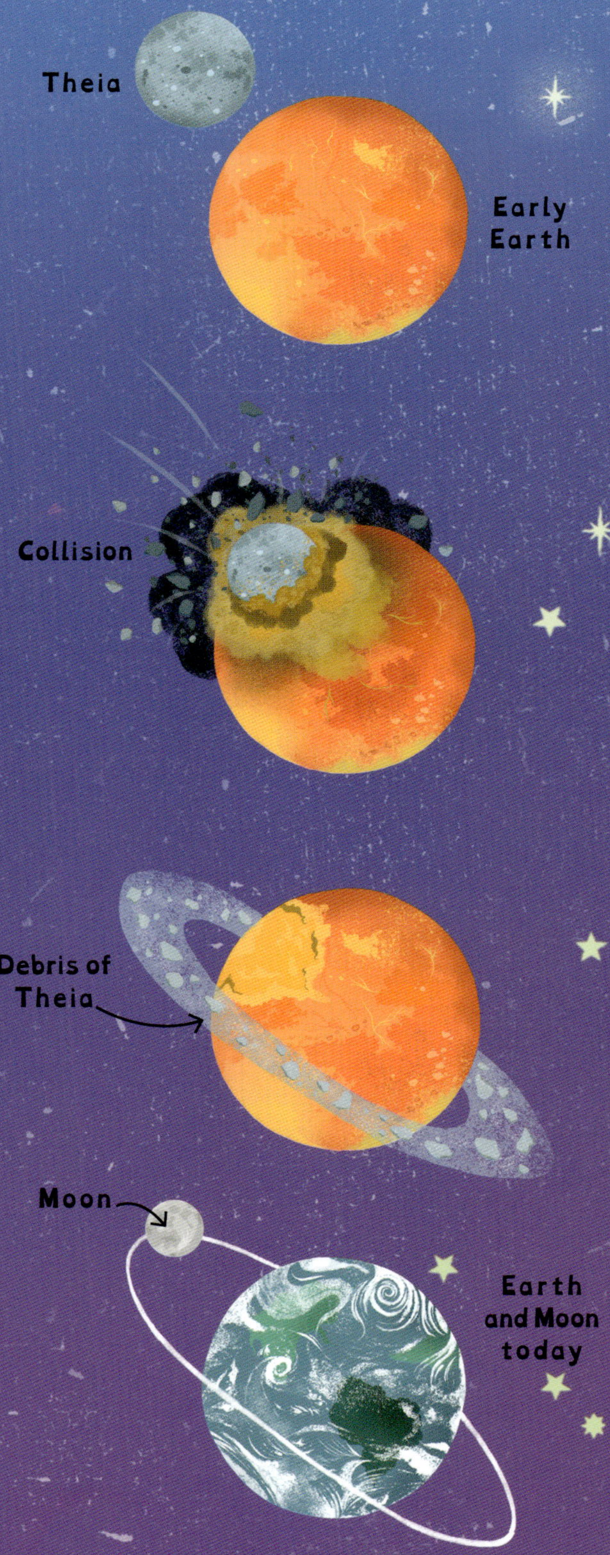

Theia

Early Earth

Collision

Debris of Theia

Moon

Earth and Moon today

First oceans

Scientists have evidence that the Earth's first oceans existed very soon after the planet's formation – around 3.8 billion years ago. The water probably came from the materials that first came together to form the Earth.

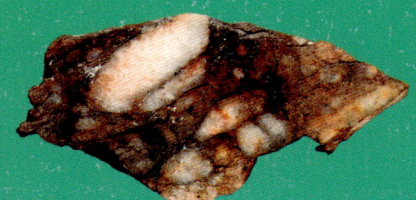

Zircons are the oldest minerals on Earth. They help geologists learn about our planet's ancient history.

Centre of the Earth

Like the middle of an apple, the deepest layer of the Earth is called the core. The Earth's core is almost 7,000 km (4,350 miles) across and lies about 3,000 km (1,850 miles) below the Earth's surface. At this depth, the temperature is incredibly high – more than 5,000°C (9,032°F), which is almost as hot as the Sun's surface!

Two parts

The Earth's core is mostly made of iron and nickel, and is split into two parts. The inner core is solid, about 2,500 km (1,550 miles) across. Sitting around this is the fluid outer core layer, which is 2,250 km (1,400 miles) thick.

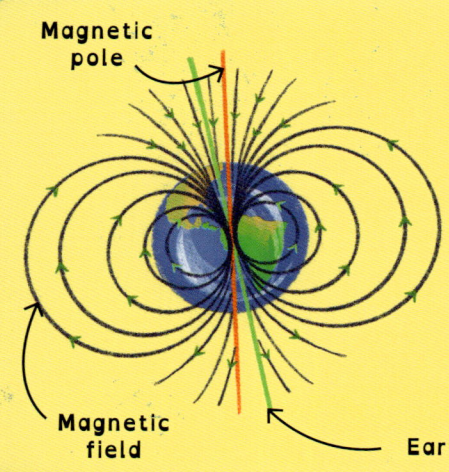

Magnetic protection

The outer core of Earth is liquid metal. The liquid metal moves in circular motions, called eddies, creating electrical currents. These produce the magnetic field that surrounds the Earth and protects our home from dangerous space radiation.

Core remains

Starting in 2029, the Psyche spacecraft will drop into orbit around the Psyche asteroid. Scientists think the asteroid is mostly made of metal and could be the remaining core of an ancient planet that was blown apart billions of years ago.

An artist's depiction of the Psyche asteroid, millions of kilometres from Earth.

Comparing cores

The InSight mission measured quakes on Mars, called marsquakes. This helped scientists figure out that the planet's core is roughly half the size of the Earth's. Mercury's core takes up the most of any planet in the Solar System – it is 85 per cent of Mercury's volume.

Core
Mercury
Mars
Venus
Earth

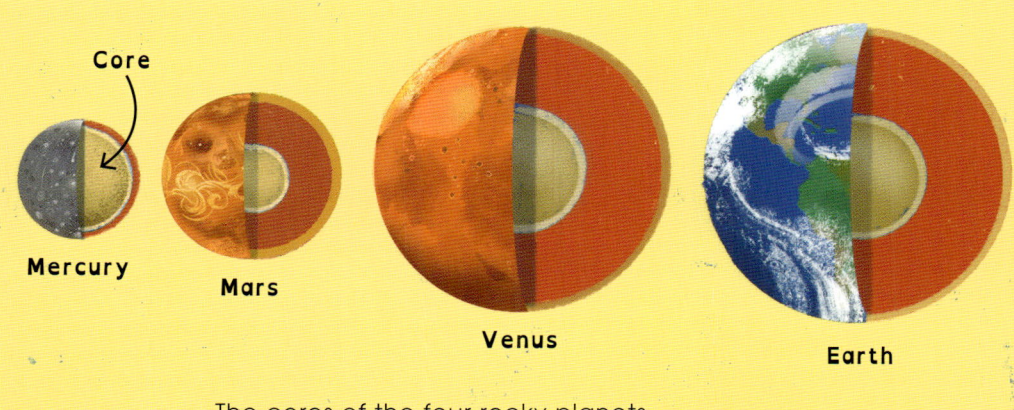

The cores of the four rocky planets

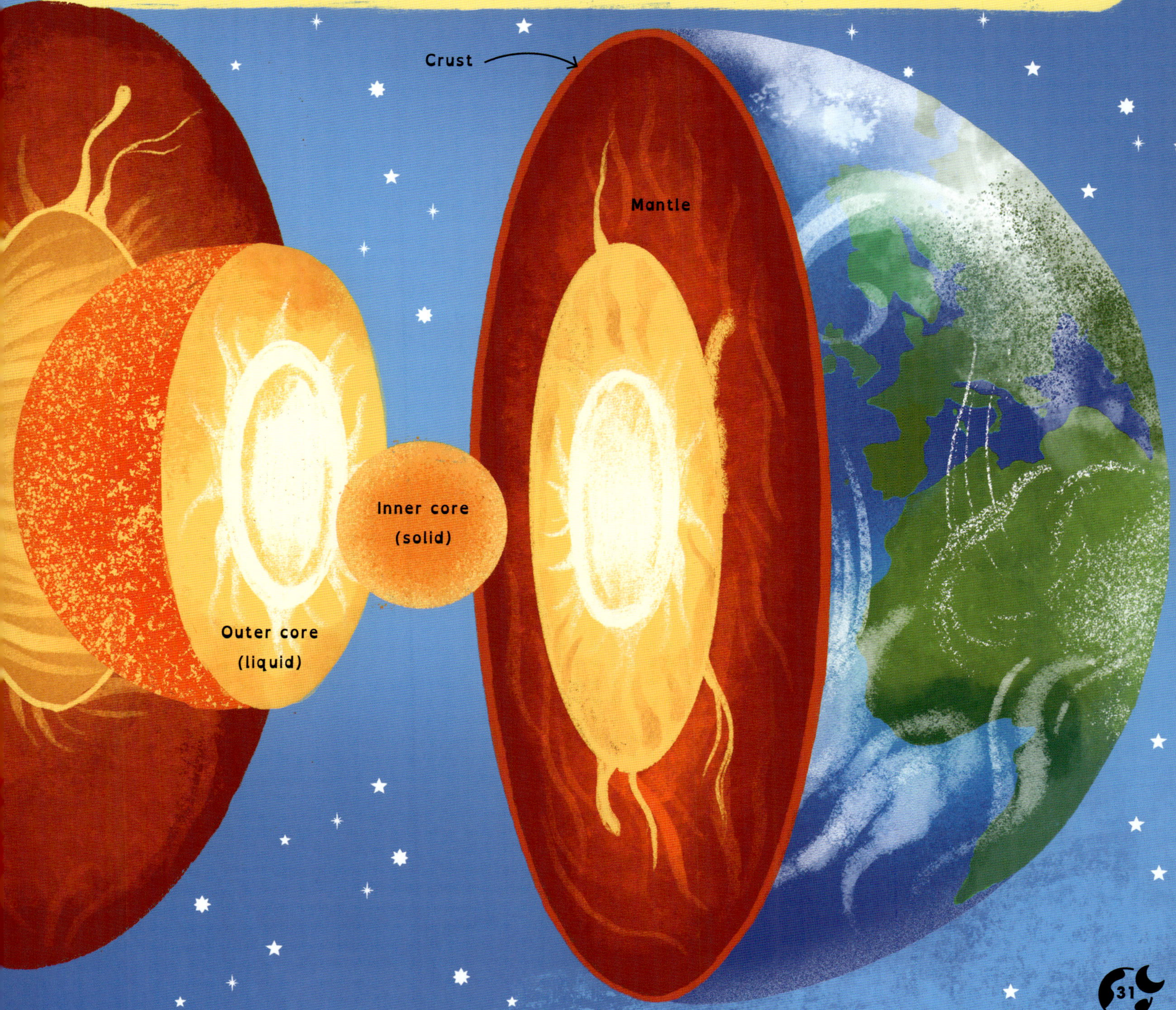

Crust
Mantle
Inner core
(solid)
Outer core
(liquid)

The mantle

The layer between the Earth's core and crust is a semi-solid rock layer called the mantle. At almost 3,000 km (1,860 miles) thick, it makes up about 85 per cent of the Earth's sphere. Because the mantle is so thick, its temperature is about 230°C (450°F) near the top but nearly 4,000°C (7,200°F) close to the core.

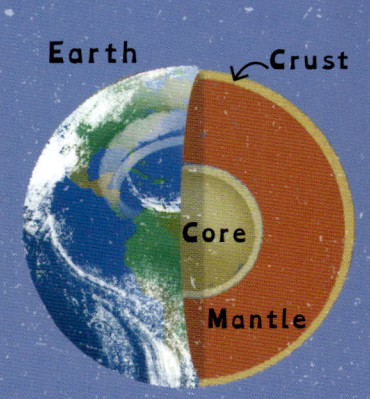

Crust

Plume head

Plume tail

Rising magma

Core

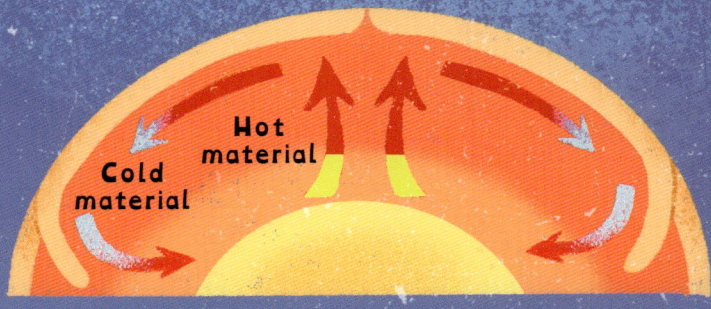

Flowing rock

Planet Earth's mantle is mostly made of rock, but it can flow very slowly like a thick goo. It moves in a circular motion, known as a convection current, where hot material moves up and cold material falls.

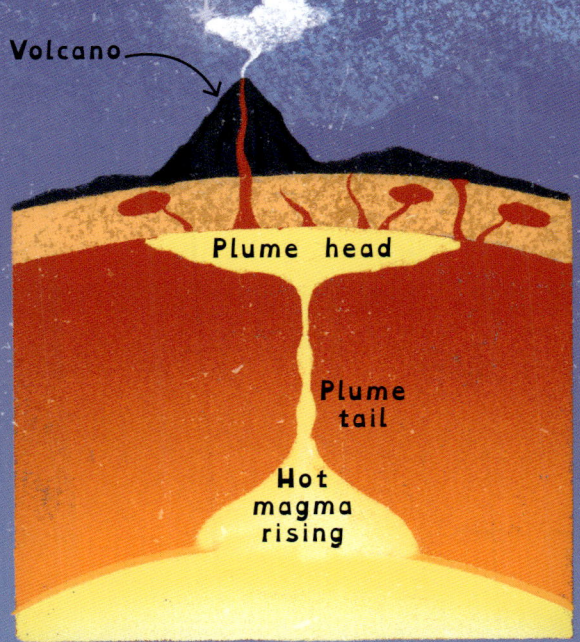

Plumes of magma

Some areas in the mantle are much hotter than others, known as plumes. Here, the rocky material melts to create magma that flows up through the mantle. Scientists think that mantle plumes cause some volcanoes, including those in Hawaii.

The boundary between the Earth's crust and mantle is known as the Mohorovičić discontinuity, or Moho.

The yellow-green parts of this basalt rock are peridotite xenoliths.

Mantle samples

It is hard to know the exact ingredients of the mantle because we can't reach it easily. Luckily, there are rocks at the Earth's surface that tell us about the mantle. For example, mantle xenoliths are pieces of solidified magma contained inside other rocks.

Mantle

The crust

The top solid layer of the Earth is the rocky crust. This is the part of the Earth that geologists can study most easily, to learn about our planet's origins and history. Although the crust is constantly formed and reformed, the oldest rocks on Earth, which are found in Canada, are ancient – 4 billion years old.

Sedimentary rocks show layers in the Earth's crust that have built up over millions of years.

Thicker and thinner

The Earth's crust is not the same all around the globe. It is made up of different types of rock and its thickness changes. The crust is thinnest under oceans, thicker under continents, and thickest under mountain chains.

Groundwater is water found under the Earth's surface, in rock and soil.

Continental crust

The continental crust is made up of layers of sedimentary, igneous, and metamorphic rocks.

20–70 km (12–43 miles)

Counting craters

The crusts of places including the Moon and Mercury are covered in craters. Like candles on a cake, the number of craters in different regions on their surfaces helps scientists work out how old these rocks are. Older rock has many craters, but newer, younger rock has fewer.

The yellow, green, and blue dots show the location of the larger craters on the Moon.

Icy crusts

Places in the outer part of the Solar System, including Pluto and Saturn's moon Enceladus, have icy, rather than rocky, crusts. The ices in their crusts are made of substances including water, methane, and nitrogen.

Scientists think that Enceladus has an icy crust on top of a warm ocean.

Water world

Earth is the only place in the Solar System with flowing water at the surface – in our oceans, lakes, and rivers. The rocks on Mars show that it had flowing water millions of years ago, but it dried up a long time ago.

Nearly one-third of the surface of Mars may have once been covered by an ocean.

River

Ocean

5–10 km (3–6 miles)

Oceanic crust

Plate tectonics

Like a jigsaw puzzle, the Earth's crust is broken up into pieces called tectonic plates. Driven by convection currents (cyclical movements caused by temperature differences) in the mantle, these plates move across the globe at about the speed fingernails grow.

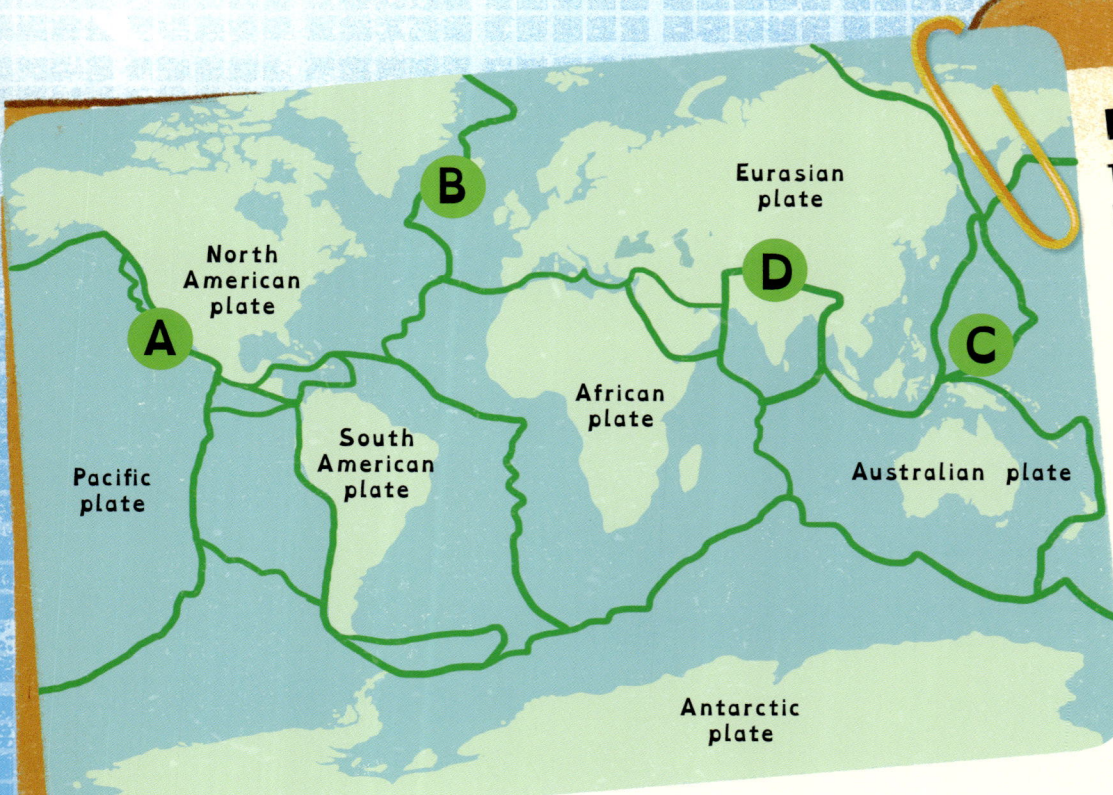

Boundaries

There are about 15 tectonic plates on Earth, eight major ones and seven smaller ones. The location where two tectonic plates meet is called a plate boundary. As the plates move, they create geological events, such as earthquakes and volcanic eruptions.

Boundary types

There are different types of plate boundaries, depending on how the plates move. A single tectonic plate can have multiple types of boundaries with the plates that surround it. Each type of plate boundary is associated with different geological features.

Transform boundaries occur when two plates move past each other in a sideways motion. An example of this is at the **San Andreas Fault (A)**.

Divergent boundaries, where plates move away from each other, create new crust between them, such as at the **Mid-Atlantic Ridge (B)**.

Convergent boundaries are where two plates collide. When this happens, one can subduct (sink) below the other, such as at the **Mariana Trench (C)**...

...or the plates at the **convergent boundary** can crumple against each other, creating tall mountains. This is how the **Himalayas (D)** were formed.

Earthquake damage to buildings in Kathmandu, Nepal.

Earthquakes

Sudden shaking of the ground, known as an earthquake, can be caused by the movement of tectonic plates. Sometimes when two plates are moving past each other, they get stuck. This creates friction, which causes energy to build up. When the plates eventually move, the energy is released, creating a shockwave that makes the ground shake. Earthquakes are most common in zones close to plate boundaries, where they can cause great damage to towns and cities.

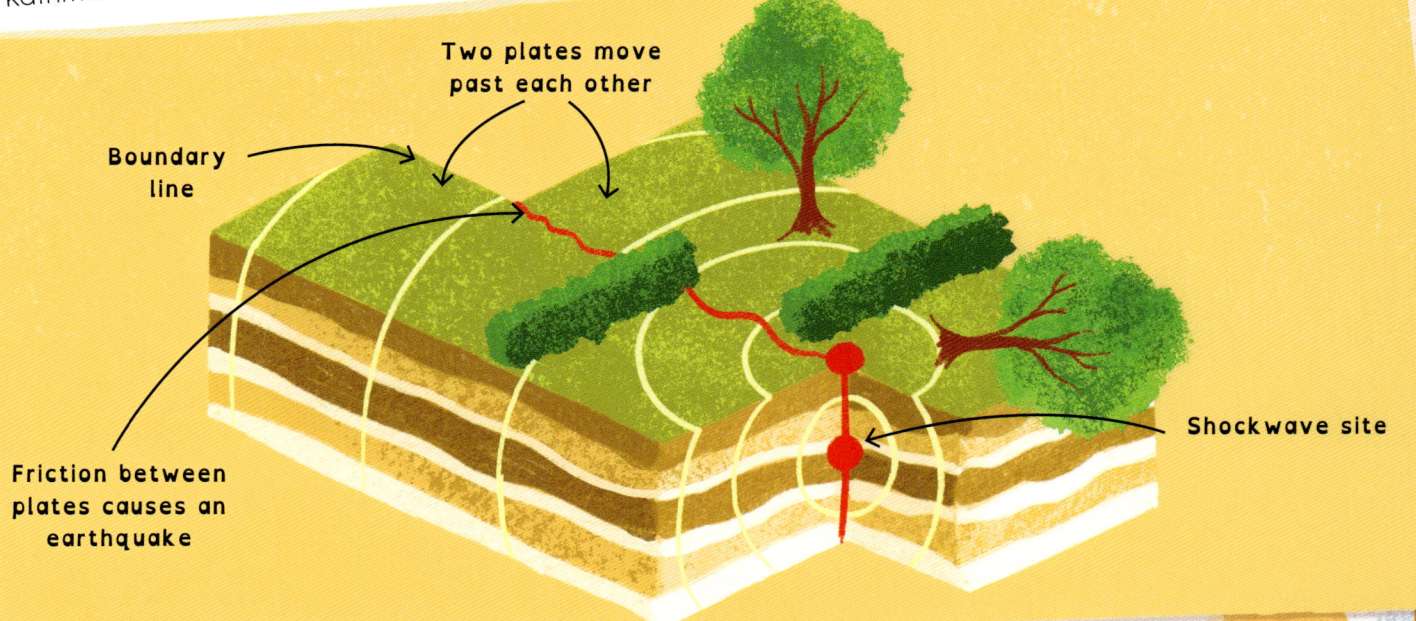

Today, Earth has seven continents: North America, South America, Europe, Africa, Asia, Australasia, and Antarctica.

Supercontinent

Plate tectonics move our continents very slowly, so the layout of the land has changed over time. Millions of years ago, Earth had a supercontinent, where most or all the land was in one piece, surrounded by one enormous ocean.

The land made a supercontinent called Pangea 200 million years ago.

Fiery start

Rocks that form when magma or lava cools, crystallizes, and solidifies are known as igneous rocks. They can form at the Earth's surface, or in the crust below. Granite and basalt are two common types of igneous rock.

Granite

Basalt

Plagioclase is the most common mineral on Earth – it is found in igneous, sedimentary, and metamorphic rocks.

The Rock Cycle

Lava erupts

Igneous rock

Magma rises, cools, and crystallizes

Changing form

As rocks move with plate tectonics, their temperature and the pressure on them can increase. Once the heat and pressure are high enough, the rocks change into metamorphic rocks, which include marble and slate.

Marble

Slate

Metamorphic rock

Magma travels up through the volcano

Mantle

Rocking around the world

There are three major types of rock found on Earth – igneous, sedimentary, and metamorphic. Changes in the Earth's crust over long periods of time, caused by plate tectonics or by erosion, can make the rocks transform into another type. This is known as the rock cycle.

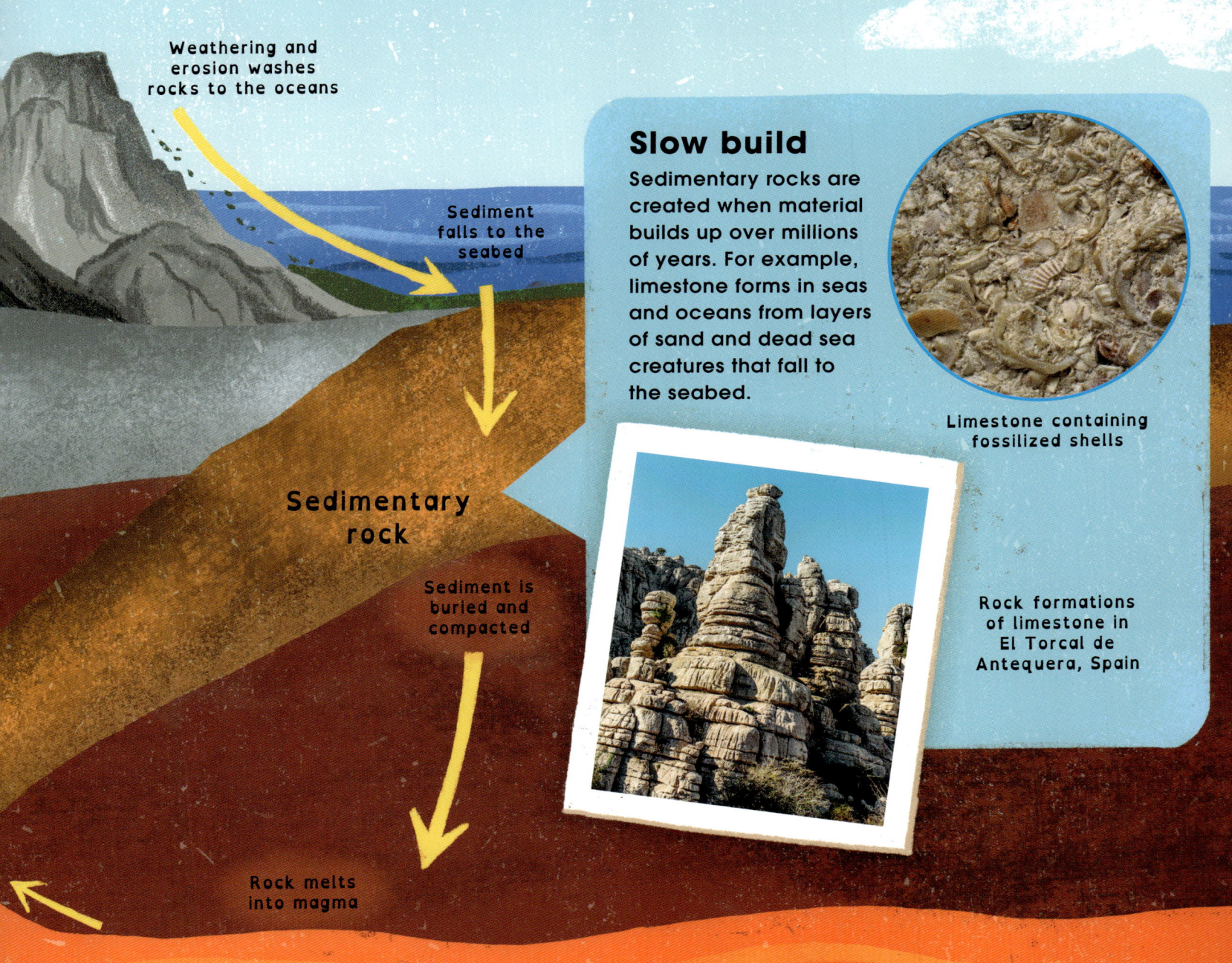

Weathering and erosion washes rocks to the oceans

Sediment falls to the seabed

Sedimentary rock

Sediment is buried and compacted

Rock melts into magma

Slow build
Sedimentary rocks are created when material builds up over millions of years. For example, limestone forms in seas and oceans from layers of sand and dead sea creatures that fall to the seabed.

Limestone containing fossilized shells

Rock formations of limestone in El Torcal de Antequera, Spain

Volcanoes

Volcanoes are openings or vents in the Earth's crust where hot magma, gas, and ash can escape. In total, there are more than 1,500 volcanoes on Earth that are active. This means they have erupted at least once in the last few thousand years. About 60 volcanic eruptions happen every year.

Ring of Fire

Many of the world's active volcanoes are found in the Ring of Fire, at the edges of the Pacific Ocean. Around this ring, the Pacific plate is pushed into the mantle and melts. This creates magma, which feeds the volcanoes.

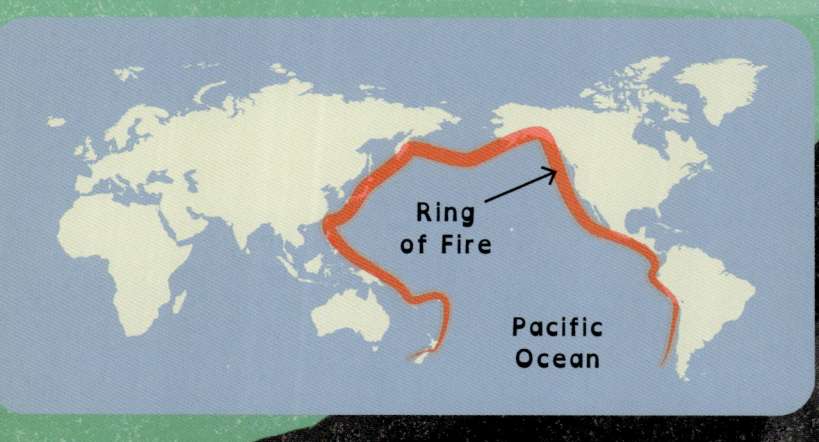

Shaping up

The shape of a volcano is normally built from several eruptions over a long time. The shape depends on the style of eruptions the volcano has. For instance, some volcanoes are shaped like wide shields and some are like steep cones.

Cinder cone Composite Shield Lava domes

The loudest sound ever recorded was the gigantic volcanic eruption of Krakatoa in 1883.

Great Volcano

The largest active volcano on Earth is Mauna Loa in Hawaii. It stands at 4,169 m (13,678 ft) above sea level. Its dome is 120 km (75 miles) long and 103 km (64 miles) wide. Mauna Loa takes up more than half of its island.

Io's volcanism

Jupiter's innermost moon, Io, has hundreds of active volcanoes, which makes it look like a pizza. Since Io's volcanism was first discovered by space probe Voyager 1 in 1979, several spacecraft have witnessed evidence including volcanic plumes rising from Io's surface.

Solar System summits

There are many summits on Earth, including volcanoes and mountains. These are often created when pieces of the Earth's crust move over each other or are squashed together. Massive peaks are also found on celestial bodies all over the Solar System.

Earth's greatest heights

Mount Everest in the Himalayas is Earth's highest peak. But the tallest is actually Hawaii's Mauna Kea volcano. Most of Mauna Kea sits underwater on the seabed, so it only rises to 4,205 m (13,796 ft) above sea level.

Mauna Kea (Earth)
10,210 m (33,497 ft)

Mount Everest (Earth)
8,849 m (29,032 ft)

Rheasilvia crater on Vesta. The red shows the highest peaks.

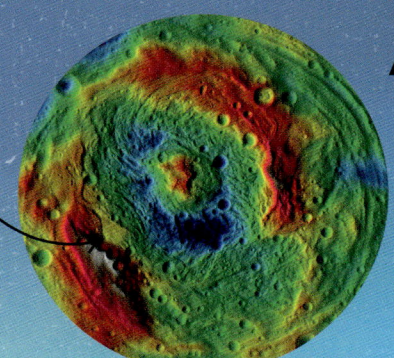

An amazing asteroid

Vesta, one of the largest asteroids, is home to a huge mountain called Rheasilvia. Rheasilvia is the central peak within an impact crater that makes up a staggering 90 per cent of the asteroid.

Rheasilvia (Asteroid Vesta)
22,555 m (73,999 ft)

Olympus Mons (Mars)
21,945 m (71,998 ft)

Mons on Mars

The peaks on Mars make Earth's summits look small by comparison. Olympus Mons is a huge shield volcano. It is the largest volcano in the entire Solar System.

Skadi Mons (Venus)
10,972 m (35,997 ft)

Very high on Venus

Like Earth, Venus has several mountain ranges. One of them, Maxwell Montes, features the tallest peak called Skadi Mons. Because of its elevation, this peak is also the coolest place on Venus – but it is still a whopping 380°C (716°F) there!

This radar image shows the Maxwell Montes mountain range in white.

Deserts

Deserts are areas where it hardly ever rains. They tend to be located in the hottest regions of Earth, near the Equator. But they are also found close to mountains, because the mountains block out lots of clouds, leaving no rain for the neighbouring land.

Big and hot

The biggest hot deserts on Earth are the Sahara in Africa, and the Arabian and Gobi deserts in Asia. But the hottest temperature ever recorded on Earth was 57°C (134°F), measured in Death Valley in the Mojave Desert of California, USA.

Some of Earth's major deserts.

Ripples are caused by wind moving the sand.

Cold and dry

The largest deserts on Earth are actually found in Antarctica and in the Arctic. The air in these places is incredibly cold and so it cannot hold much moisture. Not much life can grow there, so some of these regions look like landscapes on Mars.

A valley in the dry desert of Antarctica

Dust storms are created when strong winds sweep dust and soil from dry land into the air.

Deserts' red colour comes from the weathering of iron in the rocks.

Wind power
Many of the landforms we see in deserts – on both Earth and Mars – are caused by the power of wind. For example, sand dunes form when wind blows loose sand, which builds up into mounds or ridges.

Tumbleweeds (dried plant material) roll around in the wind, spreading seeds as they bounce along.

Dust devil

Dust devils
Several Mars missions have caught images of dust devils – or the tracks they leave behind. Dust devils are short-lived whirlwinds of fast-moving air that pick up dust and rocks. They can also been seen in deserts on Earth, but Martian dust devils are often bigger than ours.

This Mars dust devil, seen by the Curiosity rover, was about 50 m (160 ft) tall.

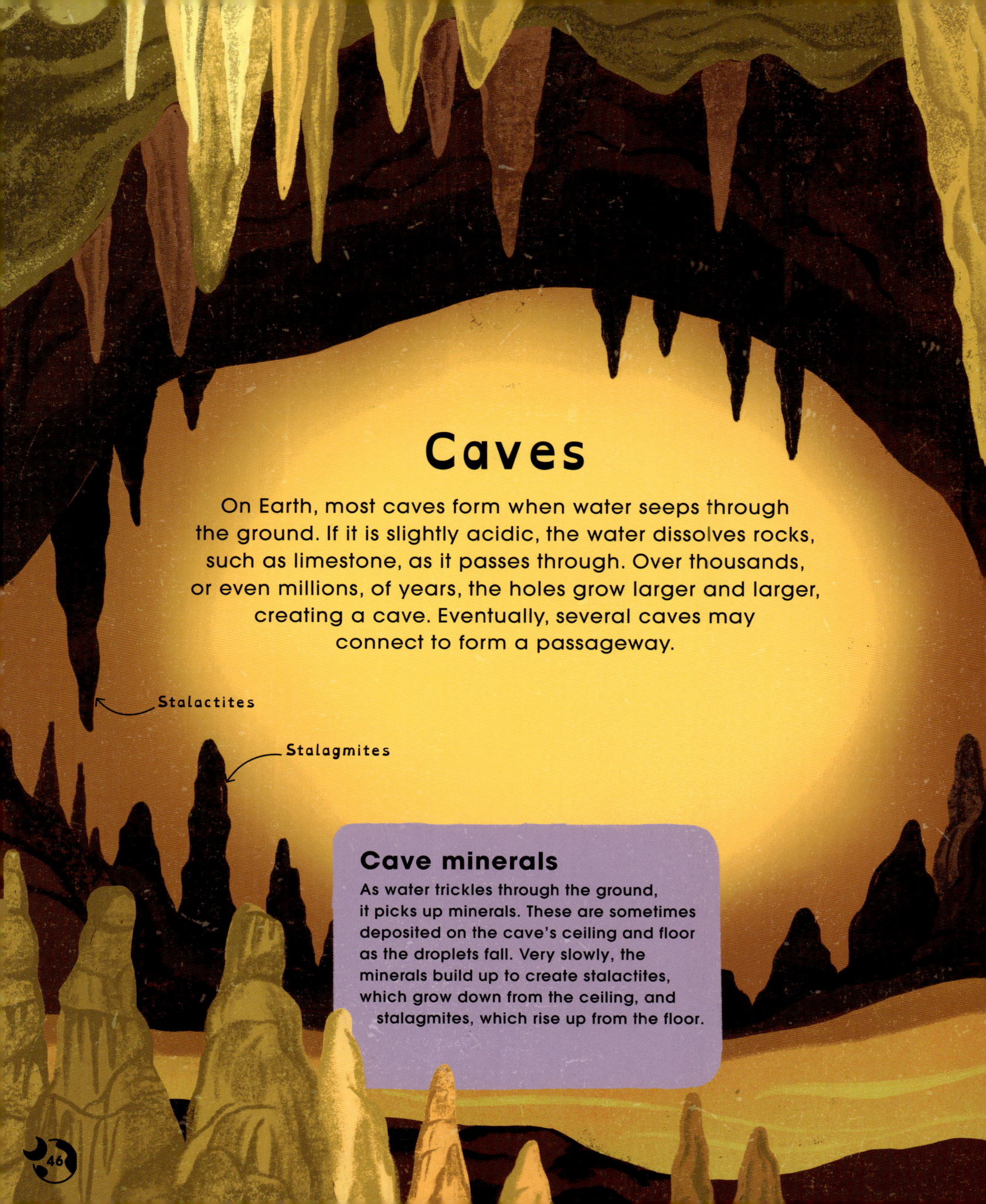

Caves

On Earth, most caves form when water seeps through the ground. If it is slightly acidic, the water dissolves rocks, such as limestone, as it passes through. Over thousands, or even millions, of years, the holes grow larger and larger, creating a cave. Eventually, several caves may connect to form a passageway.

Stalactites

Stalagmites

Cave minerals

As water trickles through the ground, it picks up minerals. These are sometimes deposited on the cave's ceiling and floor as the droplets fall. Very slowly, the minerals build up to create stalactites, which grow down from the ceiling, and stalagmites, which rise up from the floor.

Lunar lava tubes

Several caves have been discovered on the Moon. There is no water on the Moon, so these "caves" are actually lava tubes, which are formed due to volcanic eruptions. When lava cools, it can leave a hollow space with a hard outer edge. Lava tubes are also found on Earth.

Lava tube on Mount Etna, Italy

Below the surface

Across the Solar System, scientists have found thousands of holes and other clues, such as sinkholes, that might be entrances to caves. These have been found in many places, including Ceres, Titan, Pluto, Charon, and even on a comet.

Sinkhole on a comet, as seen by the Rosetta spacecraft

Martian cave dwellers?

More than 1,000 potential caves on Mars have been identified from images taken by spacecraft orbiting the planet. Some scientists think these caves would be good places for future astronauts to shelter, or may be promising places to search for extraterrestrial life.

Glaciers

Ten per cent of the Earth is covered by ice. This ice is mainly found in glaciers (thick masses of ice that flow very slowly). Smaller glaciers are found in mountain valleys, but the largest, also known as ice sheets, cover much of Greenland and Antarctica.

Glacier

Shaping the land

Due to their sheer size and weight, glaciers shape the landscapes they flow through, creating wide valleys and other features. As glaciers erode the landscapes, they also break rocks away from the ground and transport them long distances. These rocks are called glacial erratics.

This wide valley was carved out by a glacier.

Melting ice

Today, our planet is warming up quickly because human activity changes the atmosphere. This is causing glaciers across our planet to melt. In turn, the melted water makes the ocean levels rise, which causes land to flood and other major environmental problems around the world.

More than one-third of remaining glaciers are set to melt before 2100.

Ice ages

Earth's climate and temperature can change over thousands of years. Several times in the past, our world was much colder than it is today. During these episodes, called ice ages, ice and glaciers covered much larger areas of the planet.

At the height of the Pleistocene ice age, 20,000 years ago, massive ice sheets stretched over North America and Eurasia.

Earth today

Earth during the ice age

Ice on Mars

Like Earth, Mars has large ice deposits, including permanent ice caps at its poles. Mars' ice caps are a few kilometres thick and a mixture of frozen water and carbon dioxide. There is also evidence of smaller glaciers on Mars, which are covered by layers of dust or rubble.

This photograph was taken from orbit. It shows the ice cap at Mars' north pole.

Wide valley

River

Glacial erratics

Glaciers normally appear bright blue because their ice crystals are very dense and compacted.

Lakes

Lakes are large, natural bodies of water that are surrounded by land. They often contain fresh, non-salty water, but some are saltier and more like a sea. Lakes form in all kinds of places, including in volcanoes, mountain ranges, or even in underground caves.

Lake Superior

Earth's lost lakes

Over time, lakes can disappear, either due to climate changes that cause the water to evaporate, or because of tectonic shifts that drain the water. Geologists look for particular sedimentary rocks or fossils to locate where ancient, dried-up lakes once were.

Fossil fish, like this one from Wyoming, USA, show where ancient lakes once existed.

Lake Michigan

The Great Lakes

These huge lakes in North America were formed around 14,000 years ago. At the end of the last ice age, melting ice sheets revealed basins the sheets had carved into the land. These then filled with meltwater (melted snow or ice).

Martian lakes

Photographs, samples, and other information from spacecraft on Mars show that the planet's surface was once covered in hundreds of lakes. However, all Mars' lakes dried up about 3 billion years ago when the planet's climate drastically changed.

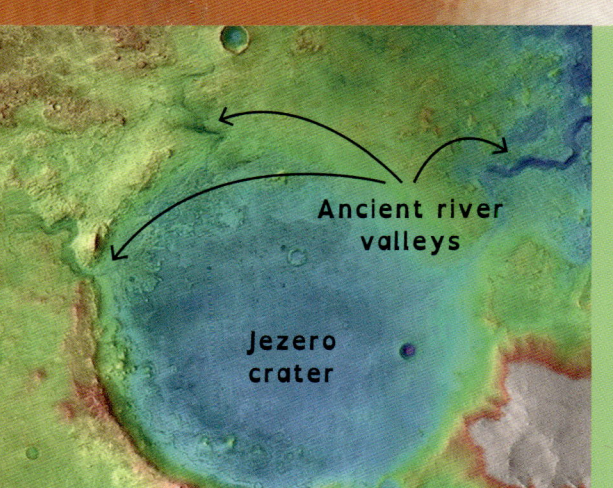

Jezero crater on Mars once held a massive lake. This map shows valleys created by large rivers, which fed the lake.

Lake life?

NASA's Perseverance rover has been exploring the Jezero crater area on Mars since 2021. The sediments left behind from the crater's dried-up lake might be the best place to find evidence of ancient microbial life (tiny living things) on Mars.

Titan's lakes

Saturn's moon Titan is the only other place in our Solar System where lakes have been found. But these lakes are not made of water! They are full of another liquid made of substances, such as ethane and methane.

Kraken Mare is Titan's largest lake.

CHAPTER THREE

THE MOON

The Moon is the Earth's only natural satellite. It is the brightest – and perhaps the most beautiful – object in the night sky.

Humans have been fascinated by the Moon for thousands of years. Many missions – human and robotic – have visited the Moon to unravel its mysteries. Scientists now understand much more about the Moon's surface and interior, but they still have many questions that remain to be answered.

Orbiting the Earth

The Moon orbits our planet at an average distance of about 385,000 km (240,000 miles). The shape of the orbit is elliptical (a slightly squashed circle). The Moon takes just over 27 days to make one complete orbit around the Earth, which is known as the sidereal month.

A special pair
Compared with other moons in our Solar System, our Moon is the largest relative to the size of the planet it orbits. In fact, the Moon is big enough to have a structure and geology that are very similar to the rocky planets.

The Moon is very slowly drifting away from Earth — a little under 4 cm (1.6 in) every year.

Phases of the Moon

The amount of the Moon we see from Earth changes over the course of a month. This depends on how much is illuminated by the Sun from our position. When it is full, we can see the whole Moon's nearside.

Same face

The Moon takes as long to spin once on its axis as it does to make one circle around the Earth. This is known as tidal locking and is the reason we only see the nearside of the Moon from Earth.

Robotic Moon missions

Humans have been sending robotic missions to the Moon since the early days of space exploration in the 1950s and 1960s. The earliest missions were basic spacecraft sent by the USA and the former Soviet Union that were designed to fly past, orbit, crash into, or land softly on the Moon.

1959 Luna 3 orbiter

1966 Luna 9

1959 Farside sighting

The first view of the farside of the Moon, which we never see from Earth, was provided by the Luna 3 mission in 1959. The blurry images taken by the spacecraft showed the farside's major geologic features.

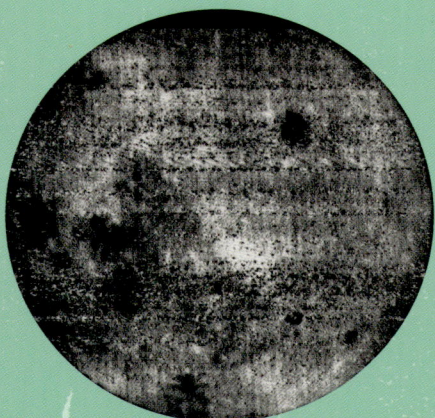

First view of the Moon's farside

1966 First landings

In 1966, the Soviet Union's robotic Luna 9 became the first mission to make a soft landing on the Moon. This was followed by NASA's Surveyor missions, five of which successfully landed. They tested the technologies needed to send humans to the Moon.

Surveyor 3 landed on the Moon in 1967

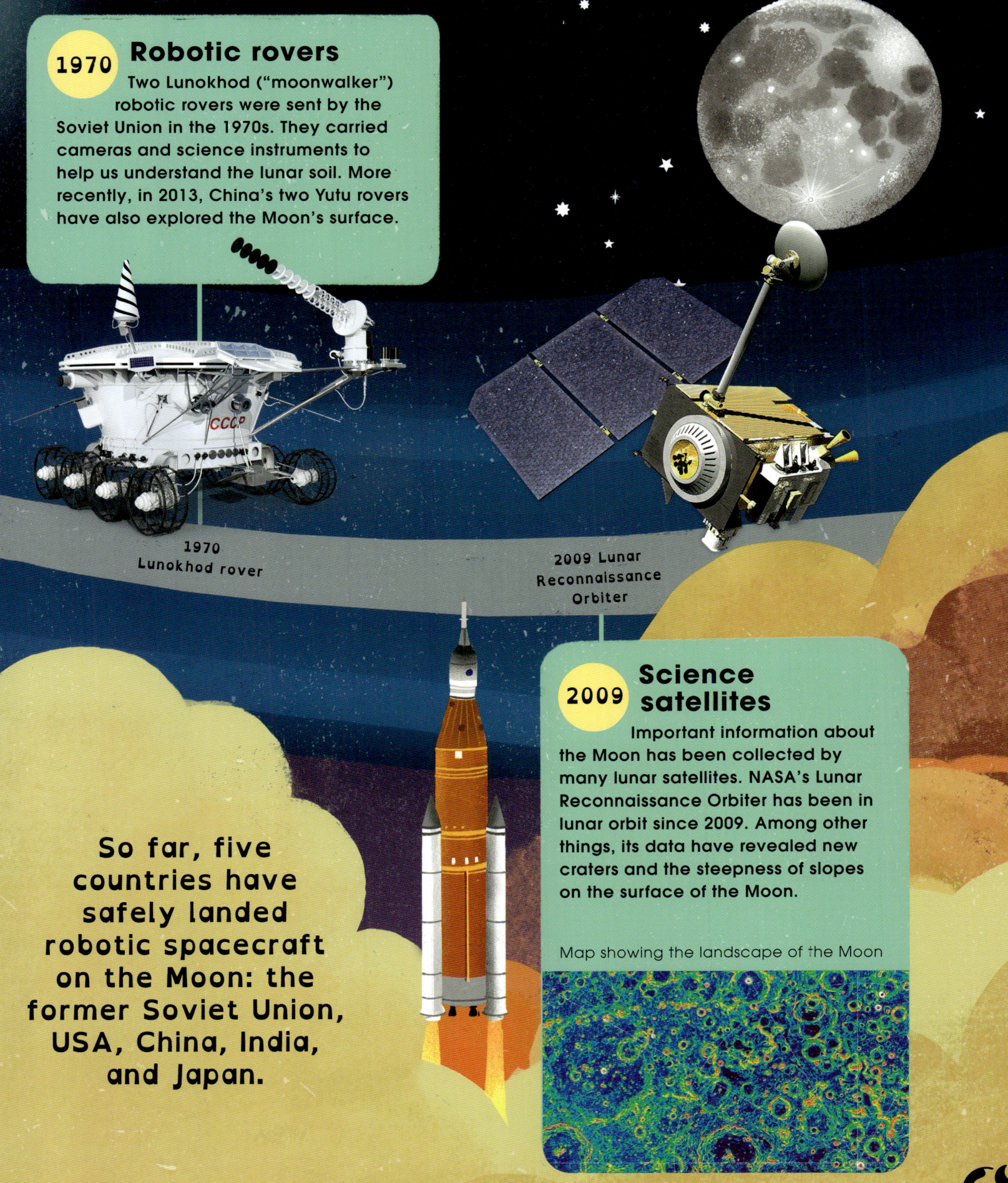

1970 Robotic rovers

Two Lunokhod ("moonwalker") robotic rovers were sent by the Soviet Union in the 1970s. They carried cameras and science instruments to help us understand the lunar soil. More recently, in 2013, China's two Yutu rovers have also explored the Moon's surface.

1970 Lunokhod rover

2009 Lunar Reconnaissance Orbiter

2009 Science satellites

Important information about the Moon has been collected by many lunar satellites. NASA's Lunar Reconnaissance Orbiter has been in lunar orbit since 2009. Among other things, its data have revealed new craters and the steepness of slopes on the surface of the Moon.

Map showing the landscape of the Moon

So far, five countries have safely landed robotic spacecraft on the Moon: the former Soviet Union, USA, China, India, and Japan.

Sending humans to the Moon

NASA's Apollo missions sent the first humans to step foot on another world, which captivated people back on Earth. From Apollo 11 in July 1969 to Apollo 17 in December 1972, 12 astronauts took photographs and conducted experiments while they explored the surface of the Moon.

Journey to the Moon

In July 1969, Apollo 11 launched on a huge Saturn V rocket. After three days, the spacecraft entered lunar orbit before the lunar module descended to the Moon's surface with astronauts Neil Armstrong and Buzz Aldrin. Astronaut Michael Collins remained in orbit and awaited their return.

Saturn V rocket

1. Launch

Apollo 11 was the first crewed Moon landing.

The command module was just over 3 m (10 ft) long.

4. Splashdown

Moon rocks were collected during the Apollo missions, which are studied by generations of geologists.

The Lunar Module was the only part of the Apollo spacecraft to land on the Moon.

2 Landing

Earth inspiration
In December 1968, Apollo 8 carried astronauts all the way to the Moon for the first time. Although they did not land there, they were the first to witness an incredible "Earthrise". They even took a photograph (above) for everyone back on Earth.

3 Return

On its return from the Moon, the Command Service Module split in two. The Apollo astronauts were sent back to Earth in the Command Module while the Service Module got left behind in space.

Successful failure
During the 1970 Apollo 13 mission, an explosion on the spacecraft meant a lunar landing was not possible. But NASA found a way to save the three astronauts and, after a week in space, they safely splashed down in the Pacific Ocean.

Apollo 13 Command Module

Inside the Moon

Like Earth, the Moon is a rocky object with a crust, mantle, and core. But there is no evidence that the Moon ever had moving plates in its crust. The Moon's mantle solidified long ago, so there is little geological activity there today.

Small core

Scientists believe that the Moon's small core is split into a fluid outer core and a solid inner core. For Earth, the same kind of core creates a magnetic field. However, the Moon does not have a magnetic field because its core is too small.

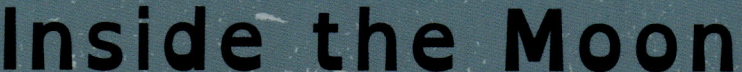

Solid inner core

Fluid outer core

Mantle

Crust

Astronaut setting up a seismometer to detect ground vibrations.

Measuring moonquakes

Seismometers left on the Moon during the Apollo missions in the 1960s and 1970s were used to measure moonquakes. Scientists used the information to work out how the inside of the Moon looks.

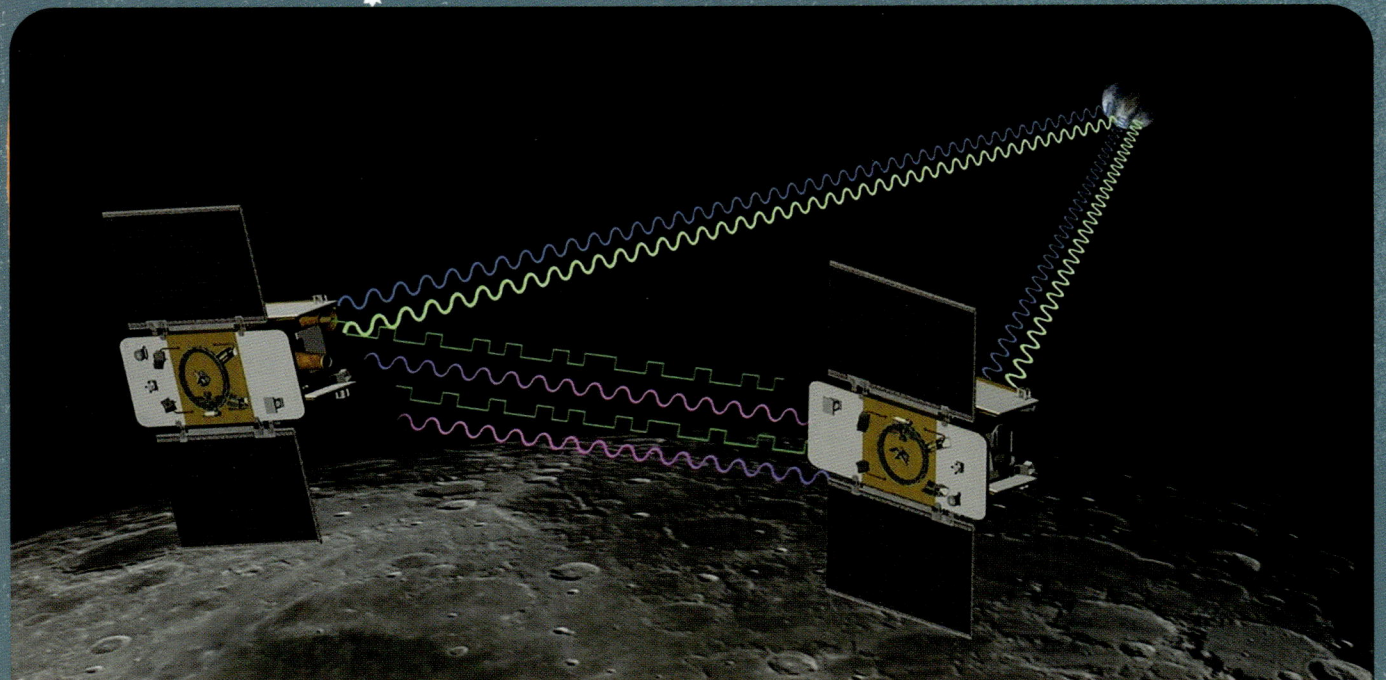

GRAIL's twin spacecraft flew in orbits around the Moon to measure its gravity.

GRAIL

Launched in 2011, NASA's Gravity Recovery and Interior Laboratory (GRAIL) mission used two twin spacecraft called Ebb and Flow to orbit the Moon and precisely measure its gravity. The results from GRAIL helped us understand how the thickness of the Moon's crust varies, and allowed the discovery of geological features below its surface.

Lasting legacy

At the end of the GRAIL mission, the two spacecraft hit the Moon close to its north pole. The GRAIL team honoured the first American woman in space by naming the site after her, calling it the Sally K. Ride Impact Site.

Sally Ride on board the Space Shuttle Challenger in 1983

The surface of the Moon

When you look up at the Moon, you see large areas of both light and dark types of rock. The light areas are mostly made of plagioclase and the dark areas are mainly basalt. We have samples of these Moon rocks, brought to Earth by astronauts and robots or delivered by meteorites.

A cratered world

The Moon is covered by millions of impact craters that are created when objects from space hit its surface. These craters have a huge range in size – the largest is about 2,500 km (1,550 miles) wide, whereas the smallest craters are microscopic.

The Moon's surface is scarred with craters.

Highlands and seas

The white areas on the Moon, called lunar highlands, are very mountainous. In contrast, the dark areas are flat and rocky. Early astronomers thought the Moon's dark patches were actually seas, so they called them "mare" (the Latin word for "sea").

Highlands (left) and mare (right)

The Moon's temperature reaches almost 130°C (266°F) in the sunlight and falls to about −150°C (−238°F) in the dark.

Moon dust

The Moon's surface is covered by a layer of tiny dust particles called regolith. This dust is created because the Moon has no atmosphere, so over billions of years continuous meteorite impacts have ground and churned up the lunar surface.

Astronaut Buzz Aldrin's boot print in the lunar regolith.

Polar ice

Although the Moon has no liquid water, there are extremely cold places near the Moon's north and south poles that are always in shadow. Scientists believe there are deposits of water ice close to the surface there, which could be a useful resource for future explorers.

Predicted ice is in blue. It is found in the darkest, coldest locations.

Lighter areas of grey show warmer zones.

Dark black areas show places in shadow, with no direct sunlight.

South pole

Finding solid ice

In 2008, the Indian Space Research Organization's Chandrayaan-1 spacecraft orbited the Moon carrying the Moon Mineralogy Mapper (M3) experiment. With M3, scientists could detect variations in light reflected from different forms of water: liquid, vapour, and solid ice.

The M3 instrument before its lunar mission.

Chandrayaan-1 spacecraft

CHAPTER FOUR

EARTH'S ATMOSPHERE

Our planet's atmosphere is essential to life on Earth.

An atmosphere is the sphere of gas that surrounds a planet and that is kept there by gravity. Earth's atmosphere provides oxygen for us to breathe and carbon dioxide for plants to thrive, and it traps heat from the Sun that stops us from freezing at night. Scientists have studied the atmosphere to understand what it is made of and how it is changing today as a result of global warming caused by humans. But Earth is not the only place with an atmosphere. Several planets, including Mars and Venus, and moons in our Solar System and beyond also have fascinating atmospheres.

What makes an atmosphere?

Earth's atmosphere is a mixture of gases: mainly nitrogen and oxygen, but with smaller amounts of other gases, including argon, water vapour, and carbon dioxide. The oxygen in the air is what we breathe to keep us alive. But Earth's atmosphere also protects us from harmful radiation coming from space.

The exosphere extends well above the official boundary of space!

Atmospheric layers

Earth's atmosphere is made up of several layers, which contain less gas as they rise away from Earth's surface. The troposphere, which is the bottom layer of the atmosphere, reaches a height of about 12 km (7.5 miles) above sea level. This layer is where most of our weather, such as clouds and wind, happens.

Exosphere
Thermosphere
Mesosphere
Stratosphere
Troposphere

Air on Mars

Mars' atmosphere is very different from Earth's. It is much thinner and almost entirely made of carbon dioxide and nitrogen, with only traces of oxygen. NASA's Mars Atmosphere and Volatile EvolutioN (MAVEN) mission has been orbiting Mars since 2014. It obtains ultraviolet images, such as these, to help track changes in the planet's atmosphere.

Mars' southern hemisphere in summer

Mars' northern hemisphere in winter

Hiding Venus

Venus' atmosphere is also completely different to that of our planet. On Venus, the dense, hot atmosphere is mostly made from carbon dioxide and nitrogen. Thick clouds of sulphuric acid blanket the planet and prevent us from seeing its surface.

Sulphuric acid droplets in Venus' clouds reflect sunlight and make the planet appear bright.

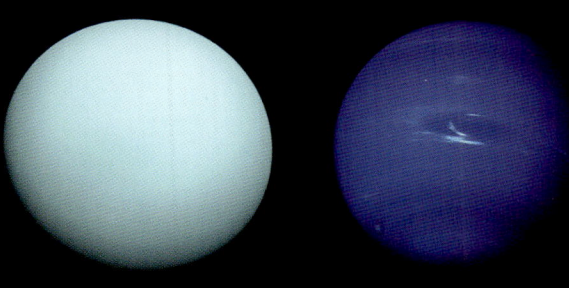

The ice giant planets, Uranus (left) and Neptune (right), have atmospheres made of the very light gases hydrogen and helium.

Ice giant atmospheres

The atmospheres of our Solar System's ice giant planets, Uranus and Neptune, are both mostly made of hydrogen and helium. However, Uranus' atmosphere is brighter than Neptune's. Scientists think this is because Uranus' has a thicker, hazy layer that whitens its appearance.

Exploring the atmosphere

Earth's atmosphere has been studied ever since the time of the ancient Greeks. But the biggest discoveries about the atmosphere only happened once scientists invented technologies to send specialized science equipment high into the atmosphere.

Pressure and temperature

Barometers and thermometers, which measure changes in air pressure and temperature, were some of the first instruments used to study atmospheric conditions. In the 1700s, explorers carried these instruments up the highest mountain in Europe, showing that temperature decreases higher in the atmosphere.

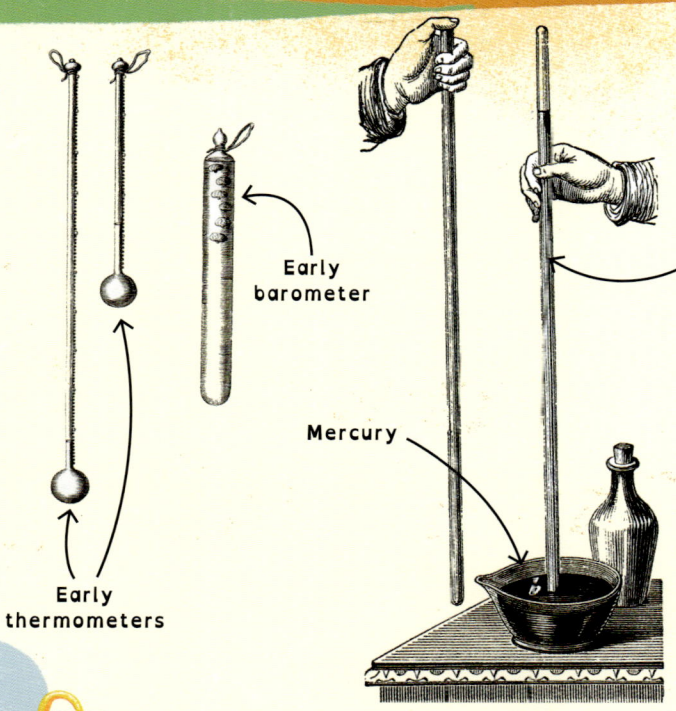

Early barometer

Glass tube

Mercury

Early thermometers

In 1643, Italian physicist and mathematician Evangelista Torricelli invented the barometer by experimenting with glass tubes filled with mercury.

Ballooning discoveries

Early scientists could make flights into the atmosphere on hot-air balloons, but there was a limit to how high they could survive. Starting in the 1890s, weather balloons – without humans aboard – were used to explore the atmosphere. These helped discover the stratosphere.

Scientist launching a weather balloon in the 1940s

Meteorologist with a modern weather balloon, called a "Jimsphere". It is used to measure wind speeds.

Rocketing research

Sounding rockets were first used for atmospheric research in the mid-1900s and are still used today. These rockets collect data during flights. They are especially useful for studying the parts of the atmosphere (mesosphere and thermosphere) that are too high for balloons to reach but too low for satellites to reach.

Journey of a sounding rocket

- Data collection
- Boom deployment
- Boom retraction
- Payload separation
- Parachute deployment
- Launch
- Splashdown and recovery

Launch of a four-stage Black Brant XII sounding rocket. This is the tallest of NASA's sounding rockets.

View from above

The outer reaches of Earth's atmosphere can only fully be studied with satellites. NASA's Global-scale Observations of the Limb and Disk (GOLD) instrument observes the atmosphere from around 120 km (75 miles) above the Earth's surface. Its data shows how the thermosphere and ionosphere (part of Earth's upper atmosphere) react to outside forces, such as solar storms.

The SES-14 communications satellite carries NASA's GOLD instrument.

Climate change

Over long periods of time, the types of weather experienced on Earth evolve – this is known as climate change. Small changes in solar activity or in the shape of the Earth's orbit can cause natural changes in climate, but human activity is responsible for most climate change today.

A warming world

Temperature measurements for the atmosphere and oceans show that Earth is currently heating up at an alarming rate. Overall, Earth's temperature has risen by more than 1°C (34°F) in the last 100 years and shows no signs of stopping.

Natural greenhouse effect

Solar heat

Greenhouse gas

Atmosphere

Heat escapes into space

Some heat trapped

Hurricanes and flooding on Antigua, in the Caribbean

Wild weather
Earth's global warming is leading to changes in our weather. Scientists expect the amount of rainfall during big storms to increase and cause more flooding. Droughts and heatwaves will also become more intense.

Working on it
Many scientists and governments are trying to find ways to reduce global warming. Actions like using renewable energy, including solar or wind power, can reduce the amount of greenhouse gases released into the atmosphere. Removing carbon from the atmosphere would also help.

Wind turbines use the force of the wind to make electricity.

Solar heat

Human-enhanced greenhouse effect

Greenhouse gases trap more heat

Less heat escapes into space

Greenhouse gases
Humans burning fossil fuels, such as gas and coal, is the biggest cause of global warming. These fuels release greenhouse gases, including carbon dioxide, into the atmosphere. These gases trap the Sun's heat around Earth, acting like the glass walls of a greenhouse. As less heat escapes into space, Earth becomes hotter.

Worlds of weather

Weather means the atmospheric conditions at any place and time. This includes all the things we notice every day, such as how hot or cold it is or if it is raining, cloudy, or sunny. A location's climate is the type of weather it generally has over a long period of time, but its weather changes often.

Earth's seasons

Earth's axis is slightly tilted, by 23.5 degrees, which creates our seasons. The northern hemisphere experiences summer when it points towards the Sun. After six months, the seasons reverse, and the southern hemisphere has its summer.

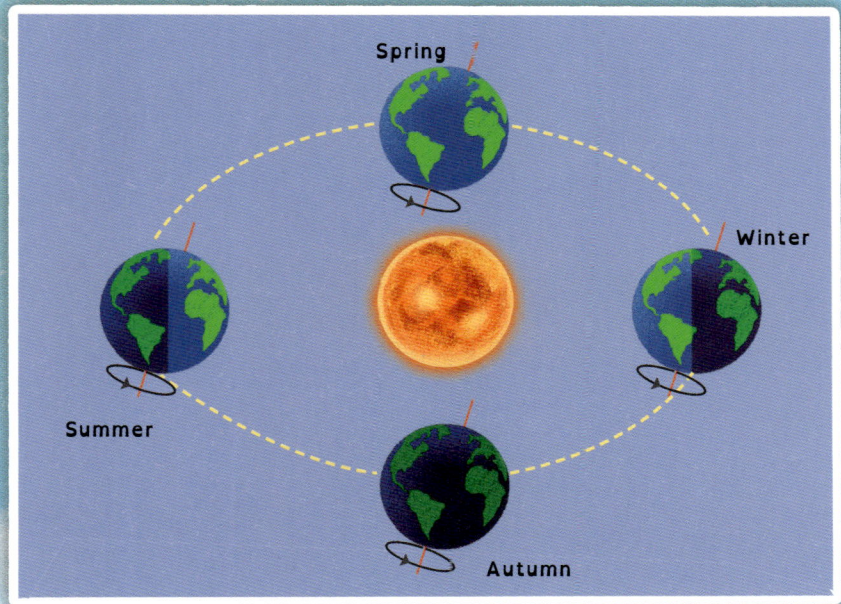

Northern hemisphere's seasons

The greatest storm

Jupiter's Great Red Spot is the largest storm in the Solar System – it is almost double the size of Earth! This storm has been spinning for more than 300 years and its winds can reach speeds of 435 kph (270 mph).

Jupiter's massive storm, known as the Great Red Spot.

Daily forecast

Data from the Mars Climate Sounder instrument on NASA's Mars Reconnaissance Orbiter is used to put together daily weather forecasts and maps of Mars' weather. These include information on the planet's pressure, temperature, humidity, and the amount of dust in its atmosphere.

Mars Climate Sounder is on the Mars Reconnaissance Orbiter

The iron oxide (rust) in the soil is blown into Mars' atmosphere by winds, which gives the sky and clouds their red appearance.

Dust clouds

Many types of clouds have been observed on Mars. One kind forms very high in the atmosphere – about 100 km (62 miles) above the ground. These high-altitude clouds form when storms cause tiny particles of Mars' red dust to be drawn up into the atmosphere.

Depiction of dust clouds on Mars at sunset.

A new home?

As the population of Earth increases, the idea that humans could live on another planet continues to fascinate people. Within our Solar System, Mars is the place we could most likely make home. But humans wouldn't survive on Mars naturally, so scientists and engineers are designing ways that could make the planet liveable.

More than eight billion people live on Earth.

You could jump around three times higher on Mars than you can on Earth. This is because the planet's gravity is much weaker.

The air that we breathe

Mars' atmosphere is thinner than Earth's and contains too little oxygen for humans to survive without breathing equipment. But an experiment on NASA's Perseverance rover demonstrated that breathable oxygen can be produced from the air on Mars.

The MOXIE experiment on Perseverance made oxygen from carbon dioxide.

Built for the cold

Mars is further from the Sun than Earth and has a thinner atmosphere. This means heat escapes from the planet easily. Temperatures on Mars rise to about 20°C (68°F), but can fall as low as −153°C (-243°F) at night. Humans would have to find ways to live in these freezing conditions.

Shields and shelters

Mars' thin atmosphere and lack of a magnetic field mean that powerful radiation from space can reach the planet's surface. This would be extremely dangerous for humans living there. Special materials and structures would be needed to shield people during radiation storms.

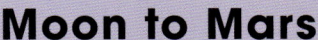

Astronauts and human habitats on Mars

Moon to Mars

Although no humans have landed on the Moon since 1972, NASA is planning to send astronauts back during the Artemis missions in the late 2020s. Humans will learn how to live and work there, and help prepare for the first human missions to Mars. Once on Mars, astronauts will make new discoveries that will help us better understand Earth.

An artist's depiction of astronaut working on the Moon during a future Artemis mission.

GLOSSARY

asteroid
Rocky object that orbits the Sun and is smaller than a dwarf planet

astronaut
Person who travels into space

astronomer
Person who studies space

atmosphere
Layer of gases around a planet or moon

axis
Imaginary line that passes through the centre of a planet or star, around which the planet or star rotates

basin
Low area of land

celestial object/body
Natural object in space located outside Earth's atmosphere, such as a star, planet, or moon

climate change
Changes in Earth's temperature and weather patterns over time, which could be natural or caused by human activity, such as pollution

core
Deepest layer of a planet or star

crater
Hole in the surface of a space object, caused by another object crashing into it

crystallize
Process of a liquid turning into solid crystals

eclipse
When an object is in the shadow of another object

Equator
Imaginary line around the centre of Earth that is an equal distance between the North and South Poles

erosion
Breakdown and movement of rock by waves, rain, or wind

ESA
European Space Agency – European organization that studies space and plans space exploration

evaporate
When a liquid becomes gas or vapour

extraterrestrial life
Any life form outside of Earth

fossil
Plant or animal, or its impression, that has been preserved in rock

galaxy
Group of star systems

geologist
Scientist who studies the history, structure, and composition of Earth

glacial erratic
Rock that has been moved by a glacier

global warming
Rise in Earth's surface temperatures due to human activities, including pollution

gravity
Force that is caused by mass, which pulls objects towards each other

ice giant
Large planet that is mostly made of gas with a layer of ice

igneous rock
Type of rock made when magma or lava becomes solid

ISS
International Space Station – laboratory that orbits the Earth, crewed by astronauts

mass
Measurement of how much matter is in an object

metamorphic rock
Type of rock formed by the action of heat and pressure on other rocks

meteorite
Remains of a meteor that lands on a planet or moon

Milky Way
Our galaxy

mission
Exploration by astronauts or robots in space

moon
Natural object that orbits a planet or asteroid

moonquake
Seismic shaking on the Moon

NASA
National Aeronautics and Space Administration – USA's agency that studies space and plans space exploration

orbit
Object's path around another object in space, such as the Moon's path around the Earth

particle
Tiny building block that forms part of an object

phenomenon
Observed event

planet
Large, spherical object that orbits a star

planetary magnetic field
Zone around a planet with a molten outer core that deflects harmful space radiation

rocky planet
Planet made up of rock

satellite
Object that orbits another object in space

sedimentary rock
Type of rock made from compressed layers of smaller fragments of other rocks, minerals, and fossils

shockwave
Wave of pressure created by fast or violent changes in pressure, such as in an earthquake

solar maximum
Period of highest solar activity in the Sun's solar cycle

Solar System
Group of objects that orbit a star, including planets, moons, asteroids, and comets

Soviet Union
Eurasian empire that existed from 1922 to 1991. Also known as USSR (Union of Soviet Socialist Republics)

star
Large sphere of gas that glows, such as our Sun

summit
Tallest point of a mountain, hill, or volcano

telescope
Tool used to look at objects that are very far away

tides
Rising and falling of the sea, due to the Moon and Sun's gravitational pull

valley
Low area of land between mountains or hills

water vapour
Gas form of water

weathering
Breakdown of rock by weather, water, chemicals, animals, or plants

Index

A
Antarctica 44, 48
Apollo missions 58–59
Arctic 44
asteroids 20–21, 30, 43, 76
astronauts 47, 58–59, 60, 75, 76
astronomers 12, 14, 62, 76
atmosphere 65–73, 76
   climate change 70–71
   exploring 68–69
   gases 66–67
   Mars 67, 74–75
   Sun 23
   weather 72–73
auroras 24–25
axis 30, 55, 72, 76

B
balloons, weather 68
barometers 68
basins 50, 76
black holes 11
boundaries, plates 36

C
carbon dioxide 65, 66, 67, 71
caves 46–47
celestial objects 9, 10, 29, 42, 76
centre of the Earth 30–31
climate 72
climate change 48, 50, 65, 70–71, 76
comets 21, 47
continents 37
core 30–31, 60, 76
corona, Sun 23
craters 20–21, 35, 43, 51, 62, 76
crust 34–35
crystallization 49, 76

D
Deimos 11
deserts 44–45
dinosaurs 21
dust 21, 62
dust clouds 73
dust devils 45

E, F
earthquakes 17, 36, 37
eclipses 22–23, 76
energy 13
erosion 39, 48, 76
ESA (European Space Agency) 21, 76
evaporation 12, 50, 76
extraterrestrial life 12–13, 47, 76
formation of Earth 28–29
fossils 50, 76

G, H
Gaia 4
galaxies 76
Galileo Galilei 14
gases, atmosphere 66–67
geology 27, 34
glacial erratics 48, 76
glaciers 48–49
global warming 65, 71, 76
gravity 10–11, 19, 61, 74, 76
Great Lakes 50
greenhouse effect 70–71
habitable zone 12
Hawaii 15, 17, 33, 41, 42
Himalayas 36, 42
hydrogen 13, 67

I, J, L
ice 35, 48–49, 63
ice ages 49
ice giant planets 67, 76
igneous rocks 38, 39, 76
International Space Station (ISS) 18–19, 25, 76
Io 41
iron 30, 45
Jupiter 11, 13, 14, 25, 41, 72
lakes 50–51
lava tubes 47
life, extraterrestrial 12–13, 47, 76

M
magma 28, 33, 40
magnetic fields 17, 24, 30, 60, 75, 76
mantle 32–33
Mars 11, 12, 31
   astronauts 18, 74
   atmosphere 65, 67, 73, 74–75
   auroras 25
   caves 47
   deserts 45
   ice 49

moons 22
volcanoes 43
water 13, 35, 51
mass 76
Mauna Kea, Hawaii 15, 42
Mauna Loa, Hawaii 41
Mercury 11, 12, 31, 35
metamorphic rocks 38, 39, 77
meteorites 20, 77
Milky Way 14, 77
missions 56-57, 58-59, 60-61, 75, 77
Moon 53-63
   astronauts 58-59, 60, 75
   caves 47
   craters 20, 35
   creation of 29
   eclipses 22-23
   interior of 60-61
   moonquakes 60, 77
   orbit 54
   phases 55
   robotic missions to 56-57
   surface 62-63
   tides 10
moons 11, 13, 14, 22, 65, 77
Mount Everest 42
mountains 42-43, 44

N, O
NASA 13, 25, 30, 51, 56-57, 58-59, 61, 67, 69, 73, 74-75, 77
Neptune 11, 13, 25, 67
nitrogen 13, 24, 66, 67
oceans 29, 48
Olympus Mons 43
orbits 22, 25, 54-55, 77
oxygen 13, 24, 65, 66, 74

P
Pangea 37
particles 21, 24, 62, 73, 77
phases of the Moon 55
phenomenon 25, 77
Phobos 11
planets 7-10, 77
plate tectonics 36-37, 38
Pluto 35, 47

R
Rheasilvia 43
Ring of Fire 40
rockets 69
rocks 34, 38-39, 58, 62
rocky planets 77
rovers 74

S
sand dunes 45
satellites 16-17, 57, 69, 77
Saturn 11, 13, 25, 51
seasons 72
sedimentary rocks 39, 50, 77
shockwaves 37, 77
Skadi Mons 43
solar flares 24
solar maximum 24, 77
solar storms 24, 69
Solar System 10, 11, 20, 28, 77
Soviet Union 56, 57, 77
spacecraft 25, 30, 41, 51, 56-57, 61, 63
stalactites and stalagmites 46
stars 4, 12-13, 14-15, 77
storms 24, 69, 72
structure of Earth 27-29
summits 42-3, 77
Sun 22-23, 24-25
supercontinent 37

T
tectonic plates 36-37, 38
telescopes 14-15, 77
temperatures
   atmosphere 68
   centre of Earth 30, 32
   climate change 70
   deserts 44
   Mars 75
   Moon 62
thermometers 68
tides 10, 77
Titan 47, 51

U, V
Universe 7, 14-15
Uranus 11, 13, 25, 67
valleys 44, 48, 77
vegetation 16
Venus 11, 12, 31, 43, 65, 67
Vesta 43
volcanoes 17, 33, 36, 38-39, 42

W, Z
water 12, 27, 35
   glaciers 48-49
   lakes 50-51
   on Mars 13, 35, 51
   oceans 29, 48
   water vapour 21, 66, 77
weather 16, 68, 71, 72-73
weathering 45, 77
weight, and gravity 11
wind 45
zircons 29

ACKNOWLEDGEMENTS

DK would like to thank Hilary Bird for the index, Laura Gilbert for proofreading, and Eleanor Bates for design assistance.

The publisher would like to thank the following for their kind permission to reproduce their photographs:

(Key: a-above; b-below/bottom; c-centre; f-far; l-left; r-right; t-top)

10 NASA: (cra). **11 NASA:** JPL-Caltech (tl); JPL-Caltech / GSFC / Univ. of Arizona (clb). **13 ESA:** NASA (bc). **NASA:** JPL-Caltech (br). **14-15 Getty Images:** Cavan / Grant Kaye (b). **14 Science Photo Library**: Rev. Ronald Royer (cra). **15 Alamy Stock Photo:** Alexandr Mitiuc (ca). **Giant Magellan Telescope – GMTO Corporation:** (cr). **NASA:** ESA and P. Goudfrooij (Space Telescope Science Institute); Processing: Gladys Kcber (NASA / Catholic University of America) (tr). **16 NASA's Earth Observatory:** (clb/x2). **NOAA:** (ca). **17 U.S. Geological Survey:** (cra). **18 Alamy Stock Photo:** NASA Image Collection (bl). **NASA:** (cla). **19 Alamy Stock Photo:** UPI / NASA (tc). **NASA:** Luca Parmitano (cr). **20 Alamy Stock Photo:** ALAMTX (cla). **21 ESA:** Rosetta / NavCam – CC BY-SA IGO 3.0 (bc). **Getty Images:** Roger Harris / Science Photo Library (crb). **NASA:** (cb). **22 NASA:** JPL-Caltech / ASU / MSSS / SSI (br/x2). **23 Alamy Stock Photo:** Zoonar / Photographer: Rolf Poetsch (cla). **24 NASA:** GSFC / SDO (bl). **24-25 Getty Images:** Moment Open / Lightcapturing by Björn Abt. **25 Alamy Stock Photo:** S.E.A. Photo / NASA (cra). **ESA / Hubble:** Hubble, NASA, A. Simon (GSFC) and the OPAL Team, J. DePasquale (STScI), L. Lamy (Observatoire de Paris) (tl). **29 Alamy Stock Photo:** John Cancalosi (br). **30 NASA:** JPL-Caltech / ASU (bl). **33 Alamy Stock Photo:** SBS Eclectic Images (crb). **34 Dreamstime.com:** Nikkytok (ca). **35 Alamy Stock Photo:** Science History Images / Photo Researchers (ca). **NASA:** Goddard Space Flight Center Scientific Visualization Studio (tl). **Science Photo Library:** M. Kornmesser / European Southern Observatory (crb). **37 Alamy Stock Photo:** GeoPic (tl); ManuelMata (br). **38 Dorling Kindersley:** Colin Keates / Natural History Museum, London (bc). **Shutterstock.com:** Yes058 Montree Nanta (cla). **39 Alamy Stock Photo:** imageBROKER.com / Moritz Wolf (cb). **40 Alamy Stock Photo:** tunasalmon (cl). **41 Dreamstime.com:** Andrii Duhin (cra). **NASA:** JPL-Caltech / SwRI / ASI / INAF / JIRAM (crb). **43 Alamy Stock Photo:** Walter Myers / Stocktrek Images (cr). **NASA:** JPL-Caltech / UCLA / MPS / DLR / IDA / PSI (tc); JPL (bc). **44 Shutterstock.com:** ENVIROSENSE (bc). **45 NASA:** JPL-Caltech / SSI (bc). **47 Alamy Stock Photo:** Alex Ramsay (cla). **ESA:** Rosetta / MPS for OSIRIS Team MPS / UPD / LAM / IAA / SSO / INTA / UPM / DASP / IDA (cra). **48 Dreamstime.com:** Beriliu (bl); Sophie Vigneault (br). 49 **NASA:** (br). 50 **James St. John:** (clb). **51 NASA:** Tim Goudge (tc); JPL-Caltech / ASI / USGS (br). **56 NASA:** (bl); JSC (br). **Science Photo Library:** Detlev Van Ravenswaay (cra, cla). **57 NASA:** (cra); NSSDCA (cla); GSFC / MIT / SVS (br). **58 NASA:** (cla). **59 NASA:** (tr). **Science Photo Library:** Carlos Clarivan (tl). **61 Alamy Stock Photo:** NASA Photo (crb). **NASA:** JPL (t). **62 Alamy Stock Photo:** NASA Image Collection (br). **Dreamstime.com:** Claudio Caridi (cla). **ESA:** SMART-1 / Space-X (Space Exploration Institute) (bl). **63 Alamy Stock Photo:** NASA Image Collection (crb). **NASA:** (tc). **67 NASA:** (cr); LASP / CU Boulder (t/x2); JPL-Caltech (bl). **68 Alamy Stock Photo:** INTERFOTO / Personalities (cra); Science History Images / Photo Researchers (clb). **Science Photo Library:** Oxford Science Archive / Heritage Images (ca); David Parker (br). **69 Alamy Stock Photo:** The Color Archives (cla). **NASA:** GSFC / CIL / Chris Meaney (clb). **71 Alamy Stock Photo:** Mike Hill (tc); incamerastock / ICP (cra). **72 Alamy Stock Photo:** Space collection (crb); Stocktrek Images, Inc. (bl). **73 Alamy Stock Photo:** Ron Miller / Stocktrek Images (br). **NASA:** JPL-Caltech (tl). **75 Alamy Stock Photo:** Futuras Fotos (br); Geopix (cr). **Getty Images:** The Image Bank Unreleased / ESA / Michael Benson (t)

Cover images: *Front:* **Getty Images / iStock:** photo5963 clb; **NASA:** cla, JPL / USGS tr; *Back:* **NASA:** JPL / USGS tl; **Science Photo Library:** Detlev Van Ravenswaay cl